Holiday

WITH MATTHEW MEAD

CREATE   DECORATE   CELEBRATE

Holiday
WITH MATTHEW MEAD

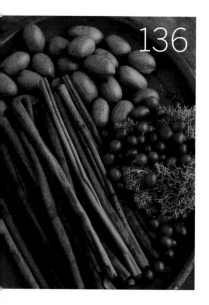

Time
HOME ENTERTAINMENT

Holiday
WITH MATTHEW MEAD

OXMOOR HOUSE

VP, Publishing Director Jim Childs

Editorial Director Leah McLaughlin

Creative Director Felicity Keane

Brand Manager Nina Fleishman

Senior Editors Rebecca Brennan, Heather Averett, Andrea C. Kirkland, MS, RD

Managing Editor Rebecca Benton

THEI

Publisher Jim Childs

VP, Strategy and Business Development Steven Sandonato

Executive Director, Marketing Services Carol Pittard

Executive Director, Retail and Special Sales Tom Mifsud

Executive Publishing Director Joy Butts

Editorial Director Stephen Koepp

Editorial Operations Director Michael Q. Bullerdick

Director, Bookazine Development and Marketing Laura Adam

Finance Director Glenn Buonocore

Associate Publishing Director Megan Pearlman

General Counsel Helen Wan

Founder, Creative Director, Editor in Chief Matthew Mead

Managing Editor Jennifer Mead

Executive Editor Linda MacDonald

Senior Writer Sarah Egge

Contributing Lifestyle Editor Stephanie Nielson

Art Director Doug Turshen

Graphic Designer David Huang

Studio Assistants/Designers Lisa Bisson and Lisa Smith-Renauld

I would like to thank everyone that helped to make this special volume of HOLIDAY 2012 very merry, including: Emilie Ash, Amy Barickman, Georganne Bryant, Bradford Crowder, Debbie Dusenberry, Mary Engelbreit, Maggie Grussing, Justin Hackworth, Michelle Leiter, Sally McElroy, Darryl Moland, Debra Norton, Penacook Historical Society, Lee Repetto, Stefanie and Luke Schiada, Carol Spinski, Paul and Lianne Stoddard, Koralee Teichroeb, Mary and Gordon Welch, Kate Wheeler, Stacey Willey, my amazing team, and all the wonderful support from Julie Merberg and the team at Time Home Entertainment, Inc.

With any craft project, check product labels to make sure that the materials you use are safe and nontoxic. The instructions in this book are intended to be followed with adult supervision.

NOTE: Neither the publisher not the author is responsible for your specific health or allergy needs that may require medical supervision, or for any adverse reactions to the recipes contained in this book.

ISBN 10: 0-8487-3814-4
ISBN 13: 978-0-8487-3814-3

editor's letter

I GREW UP IN THE 1970'S in a modern-style ranch house. While it wasn't large, it was someone's idea of how modern American families could live together in efficient, comfortable surroundings for less. For Christmas, we set up a cardboard chimney and fireplace from which to hang our stockings and provide a portal for jolly St. Nick. I was completely enchanted by it and all of the ceremony and fun of setting up this holiday scene and planning for the arrival of Christmas. Looking back as an adult, I now see that this humble, faux fireplace was part of the building blocks for my imagination. It allowed me to dream about the holidays in the most vivid and colorful ways, and opened my mind to the idea that even a cardboard facsimile could deliver as much joy as the real bricks and mortar version. And so began the journey for my life as a designer, stylist, and author, and I continue to conjure up many special and imaginative ways to experience the holiday season. I hope that what I have created here, in the pages of this volume, allows you to dream beyond the pictures and ideas to make your own special projects and memories. And when you don't have exactly what you need to recreate the scene? Take a page from my childhood holiday and improvise; you just might unleash your own special brand of festive flair!

Merry Christmas and Happy Holidays,

Keep up with HOLIDAY and all of our seasonal pursuits at HolidayWithMatthewMead.com

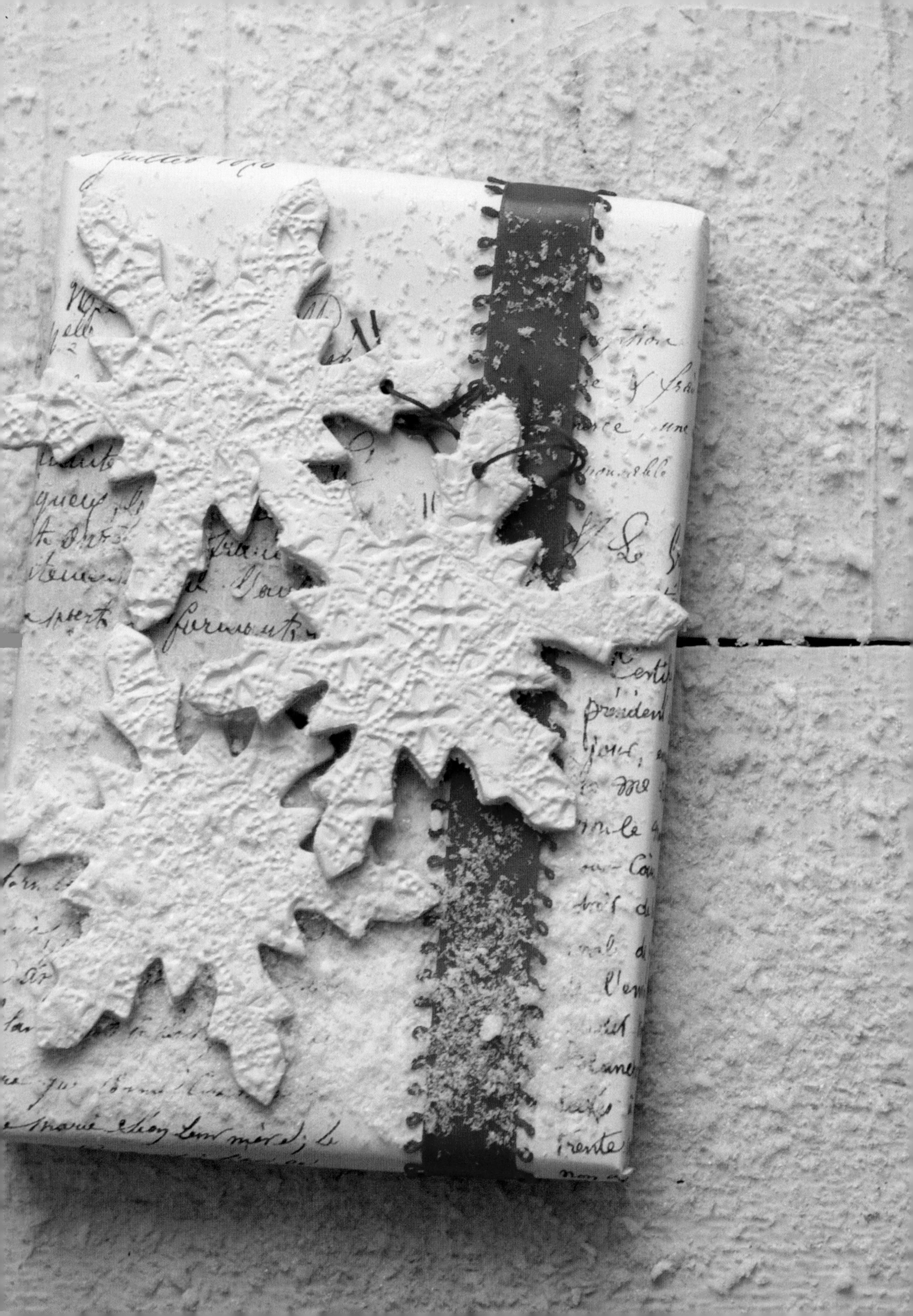

CREATE

Every year my mind overflows with a million ideas for the holiday season. I love making ornaments and cookies and all kinds of wreaths for the house, but mostly I enjoy gathering my family and friends to help. We assemble ingredients and supplies, walk the yard clipping fragrant evergreens, and visit our town's old-fashioned candy store to get mouth-watering novelties for embellishing cookies and topping gift packages. For me, these rituals are part of the build up to Christmas— they are the traditions that I look most forward to. Creating things and creating memories are one in the same.

WINTER WREATHS

Wrapped in tradition, these enduring wreaths will welcome guests straight through the season. Gather a few simple supplies and make your own colorful greeting.

FRESH ADDITIONS Holiday wreaths can be made in a variety of shapes, sizes, and materials. Create a textural star wreath (this page) using a wire wreath form, ribbon, and a mix of walnuts, hazelnuts and almonds. Wrap the wreath form with ribbon and hot glue nuts to the ribbon in a random pattern. Hang with evergreen garland or simply wire the star form to a lush green wreath for a natural finish. **OPPOSITE:** Dress up a fresh pine wreath with berry sprays, cuttings of variegated euonymus, and blooms of purple anemones fitted with water picks to ensure freshness. As needed, remove spent blossoms and replace with flowers of a different color palette for interest and new color.

BERRY ABUNDANCE Purchased at a garden center, a terra-cotta wreath (this page)—with a berry and pomegranate motif—is painted using red and white acrylic paints and then white-washed with glaze. This type of wreath will last from year to year and can be painted in any color scheme you desire; we chose a classic Scandinavian palette of red and white.
OPPOSITE: A mix of fresh or faux holly, rose hips, tallow berries, and juniper are wired to an oval-shaped twiggy form to create a colorful wreath for any spot in your home. Gather an ample supply of berries and greens and attach to the form using floral wire. Finish the wreath with a flourish by hot-gluing sprigs of extra-special berries into place.

SILVER THAW A wreath of faux laurel leaves, glittered in silver, stands up to wintry weather (this page). To make, weave four branches around a wire form and secure using floral wire. The monochromatic scheme highlights the shape and texture, creating an everlasting sparkle effect that catches the sun's light during the day and reflects the twinkle of Christmas lights at night. Hang this wreath on an outside gate, door, or window. **OPPOSITE:** Embellish a twiggy wreath with icy embellishments, like a selection of frosted faux branches and a mix of pine cones sprayed with artificial snow. Use hot glue to attach each element and arrange the branches in a random, natural fashion.

CITRUS AND GREENS A circle of dried lotus pods is nestled around a fresh boxwood wreath (this page) for a striking woodland effect. Hung against an aged pine door, the pairing strikes a perfect balance of color and natural rusticity. Purchase the boxwood wreath form at a flower shop and look for dried lotus pods in the faux flower section of most craft stores. Use hot glue to secure the pods to the wreath and attach sturdy wire to the back of the form for hanging. **OPPOSITE:** This fragrant and colorful fruit wreath is created using oranges and lemons that have been skewered with floral picks and tucked into a fresh wreath made with lush lemon leaves. Hang indoors in a cool, dry place for up to 10 days.

STORYBOOK CHRISTMAS

From gift wrap to table
decorations, candy confections
can sate your sweet tooth
and so much more.

ON THE SWEET SIDE Form a jolly centerpiece with an army of kitted-out snowmen (above) marching across a platter of fake snow. Drop dollops of boiled icing on a cookie sheet to create bodies and heads. When the dollops are set, stack them, wrap scarves of fruit ribbon around their necks, and make faces using cookie decorations. For their hats, top a circle of fruit ribbon with a red gumdrop. Hold it all together with dabs of royal icing. *Note: Fake snow is not edible.* Fashion a wreath (opposite) by piping a ring of homemade or store-bought royal icing around the edge of a plate. Anchor gumballs and a ribbon bow in it, and let the icing set. Log onto HolidayWithMatthewMead.com or see page 234 for boiled icing and royal icing recipes.

FESTIVE EDIBLES **1.** Invite little ones to a tea party, serving up truffles and cookies dipped in white chocolate and crushed peppermint candies. Pour little sippers of white cocoa into votive candleholders. **2.** Treat-filled poppers are easy-to-make party favors. The pattern is on page 246 and at HolidayWithMatthewMead.com. Wrap the paper around cardboard tubes, fill with candies, and tie the ends with ribbons. **3.** Festoon wrapped packages with melt-away decorations, from barley candy letters to sugary Santas. Stick the treats to the packages with dots of royal icing or crafts glue. **4.** For an edible snow globe, tuck a boiled-icing Santa into a tall drink glass filled with candy snow, which you can purchase at a cake-decorating store.

TASTY TEAMWORK
Crafting queen Mary Engelbreit
(MaryEngelbreit.com) turned
recyclables into a fairyland for
Matthew's candy creations. Follow
her lead to cover tins and potato-
chip containers with scrapbook
papers and ephemera. Pipe on
icing frills. Then "landscape"
with artificial snow, boiled-icing
snowmen, and fondant toadstools.

ICING ARTISTRY To make this sweet Father Christmas, pipe red-tinted boiled icing following the pattern on page 246. When hardened, add arms. Tint more boiled icing (the recipe is at HolidayWithMatthewMead.com and on page 234) for face, beard, and hands. Then use cake and cookie decorations and fruit rubber to add buttons and trimmings.
OPPOSITE: Like an artist who works with a paint palette, ply candy to cutout ginger cookies to turn them into personalized tree ornaments. Frost cookies with royal icing, and then embellish them with fondant shapes and sugary baubles before the icing sets. If you don't eat them all, thread a rickrack ribbon tie through the hole and hang the ornaments on the tree.

ANGELS

Heralding the holiday, angels infuse your home
with a comforting spirit. Decorate with collectibles from
flea markets, and embellish with their motifs.

CAPTURE THE MOOD
Give new life to a glass paperweight (this page). Scan in a vintage letter to use as the background, add an elegant script message, and print it in color. Adhere the paper to the paperweight with ModPodge® découpage medium. An airy birdcage (opposite) is a showcase for a vintage plaster plaque depicting a guardian angel.

"Angels evoke the very best of the season. Jenny and I like to sprinkle them throughout the house." — *Matthew*

HEAVENLY DESSERTS Elevate a spicy, rich ginger cake to a special-occasion confection by topping the cream cheese frosting with an angelic motif. Lay down a stencil, which you can trace on page 246 and cut from paper. Dust the entire cake with ground cinnamon, and then remove the stencil to reveal the pattern. **OPPOSITE:** Before baking a batch of gingerbread cookies, poke holes in their shoulders using a bamboo skewer. When baked and cooled, use cooking twine to tie on paper-cutout wings; the pattern is on page 248 and at HolidayWithMatthewMead.com. Note: You can find the cake and cookie recipes at HolidayWithMatthewMead.com or on page 234.

HEARD FROM ON HIGH Cut angels from stiff paper or card stock (the pattern is on page 247) and stamp family members' names on them to create perennially elegant mantel decorations or dinner place cards. **BELOW:** Long ago separated from their dresser drawers, these fanciful handles take on the look of angel wings with a coating of white spray paint. Use them to corral napkins. **OPPOSITE:** Complement milky Bristol glass vases by adding pairs of angel wings. Cut the wings from paper (the pattern is on page 248), then use white crafts glue and gold glitter for highlights. When dry, tape them to the back of the vases. For extra atmosphere, sprinkle in feathers and a package wrapped in gold jewelry wire and a bauble from the crafts store.

1

2

3

WINGED CREATURES

Pure white collectibles and gold embellishments mix easily into your holiday décor, giving your rooms touches of serenity and calm. **1.** Jenny became fascinated with angels after reading a book about real-life angel encounters. Her interest spurred Matthew to build a collection for her from flea-market finds, including pieces such as this ceramic pitcher with an embossed angel motif. **2.** Repurposing a bit of old lace, the edge of a stained tablecloth, or a vintage hankie, fashion an angel to decorate a gift box. Follow this example, which Matthew and Jenny place around the table at a holiday brunch. **3.** Matthew likes to mix angels with a few gold metallic Syroco pieces—hot items at flea markets and estate sales. The ornate, molded-resin accessories, which date back to the early 1900s, fit right into this majestic wall tableau. On a rustic curtain rod mounted to the wall, string gilded molding details, including a Syroco wall pocket. Tuck in a hand-written letter, and add a set of wings from a child's costume. **OPPOSITE:** In the luminous panes of a salvaged window, place angel depictions borrowed from a box of artful note cards. Scan and print the angels onto vellum paper, cut them to fit the windowpanes, and attach them with spray adhesive.

ALL THAT GLITTERS

Prepare to get your sparkle on as Linda MacDonald, author of the popular blog *Restyled Home*, shares easy-to-make glitter projects that reflect her home's signature holiday style.

ALL WRAPPED UP (THIS PAGE): A designated wrapping station is bedecked with projects Linda created for the holiday season. Set against a checkerboard backdrop of glittery 12x12-inch scrapbook paper—adhered using low-tack tape—the station is both pretty and functional. Linda then applied glittered trees to the empty spaces on the wall between each paper square. To make, first download and print the tree patterns at HolidayWithMatthewMead.com. Trace the patterns onto sheets of 12x12 glittered scrapbook paper. Cut out the shapes and apply hot glue to the back of the smaller tree and adhere it to the front of the larger tree.

SHOPPING LIST (OPPOSITE): Glittered ribbon has a myriad of uses during the holidays, beyond just dressing up packages. Purchase the glitter ribbon, scrapbook papers, and Zots™ glue dots at crafts stores, such as Michaels.

GLITTER AWAY 1. Linda uses glitter liberally when crafting. In addition to creating new glitter projects each year, she repurposes outdated holiday décor with glitter in her favorite shades. **2.** Small vintage light bulbs are given new life and sparkle, again using Mod Podge® and glitter. Linda wrapped florist's wire around each bulb's base for easy hanging on a tree or to adorn a garland or wreath. **3.** Edible glitter is sprinkled on frosted cupcakes to provide sweet nourishment during busy craft sessions. **4.** Use a 12x12-inch glittery scrapbook paper as an impromptu place mat. Cut a 2x8-inch strip of the same paper to make a napkin holder for each place setting. Adhere the ends together using hot glue and wrap a narrow strip of glittered ribbon around the holder; secure using more hot glue.

ON A PEDESTAL

A tiered stand holds a tempting array of holiday treats and shimmering décor. Linda filled a collection of vintage glasses with candied almonds, and nestled cupcakes and cellophane-wrapped sweets on each tier. With her three children in-house, the treats won't last long. She hung the glittered light bulbs from each level by simply bending the wire to form a hook that is used to secure each bulb into place. This garland effect adds sparkle and color to the display. Glittered trees (see templates on page 250) stand tall with the aid of small votives. Use Zots™ to secure the trees to the (unlit) votives. Linda likes to incorporate prettily wrapped gifts into her holiday décor. She wraps an assortment of hostess gifts and sets them below the stand for easy access when heading out to holiday gatherings.

"I love using glitter. It just makes me happy." — *Linda*

TREE OF LIGHT

"Not every tree has to be real," suggests Linda. Look beyond the walls of your home and adorn a window with shimmery candle decorations (this page). Using several colors of glittered scrapbook paper and the candle template found on page 250, cut out the patterns and adhere each piece in place with hot glue. Using clear tape, attach the candles to the window and apply them in a tree shape, spacing each tree about 1 to 2 inches apart. The result is an eye-catching holiday display that, combined with Linda's color palette, offers a break from tradition.

ALL THAT GLISTENS

Scrapbook-paper glitter pockets—filled with fresh greens, glittered light bulbs, and candy—hang in a trio on a wall (opposite), ready to be pressed into service as last-minute holiday gifts if needed. Linda dusted the greenery (artificial may also be used) with faux snow and tied on a pretty bow using the leftover glitter ribbon from other projects.

To make the pockets, use the template on page 251 and follow the directions found on our website, HolidayWithMatthewMead.com. For a fun, take-away holiday party favor, fill with your guests' favorite sweets, ornaments, or small trinkets and hang from the back of their chairs.

"Glitter casts a magic spell, instantly transforming the ordinary into something special." — *Linda*

1

2

3

4

1. GLITTERED CONE MEDALLION

Make in a variety of colors and hang in groups over your holiday table.

You will need:

- 3 sheets of 12x12 glittered scrapbook paper
- Cone template (found on page 251)
- A sheet of heavy cardstock
- A stapler
- Glue gun
- Hot glue sticks
- A ¹⁄₁₆-inch hole punch
- Clear monofilament wire

1. Roll the cone template and secure using a stapler.

2. Cut a 3½-inch cardstock circle.

3. Arrange the 13 cones on the circle and adhere using hot glue.

4. Cut a 2-inch and 1-inch circle from the glittered paper, and glue the smaller circle to the large. Apply hot glue to the back of the large circle and adhere to the center of the medallion.

5. Using a hole punch, create a small hole at top of medallion, string with clear monofilament line, and hang from a window frame or ceiling.

2. FESTIVE RIBBON CHAINS

Make this glittered ribbon version of childhood gum wrapper chains, and use them to dress up glassware.

You will need:

- 4-inch x 1-inch lengths of glittered ribbon (as many as you need to create the length desired)
- Glue gun
- Hot glue

1. Fold in half along the length of the ribbon.

2. Fold each end to the middle.

3. Fold in half along the ribbon length again.

4. Fold entire ribbon in half.

5. Fold the ends in half towards the middle so that they meet.

6. Repeat with another length of ribbon.

7. Now with two links, fit the loop ends through one another.

8. Repeat the process, adding additional links until you reach the desired length of chain. Hot glue the ends together.

9. Wrap each chain around a glass or votive.

3. SPARKLY RIBBON-WEAVE GIFTS

This elegant gift wrapping idea is pretty enough to make presents take center stage underneath a decorative table-top tree.

You will need:

- Plain, colored gift wrap
- Several spools of glittered ribbon (measure lengths to fit each package)
- Glue gun
- Hot glue

1. Wrap each package using the plain, colored wrapping paper.

2. Beginning at the center, run a length of ribbon around the package and fold down the ends of the ribbon and glue their edges to the underside of the box using hot glue.

3. Using these ribbon patterns as a guide, weave the other ribbons through each other, continuing to secure to the underside of the gift.

4. SHIMMERED-RIBBON CANDLE BOOKMARK

Make several to tuck into books for holiday gifts.

You will need:

- 18-inch length of 1-inch glittered ribbon
- Glue gun
- Hot glue
- 3-inch length of narrow, glittered ribbon

1. Pleat and flatten the wider ribbon, securing each pleat with hot glue.

2. Make a V-snip at bottom of ribbon.

3. Hot glue each end of narrow ribbon to the top back of the candle to form the flame.

CANDY
PAPER
SCISSORS

Stephanie Nielson and her children draw inspiration from holiday candy to create a spectacular handmade Christmas using an assortment of pretty papers and a tempting array of sweets.

LIFESTYLE PHOTOGRAPHY BY JUSTIN HACKWORTH

ALL STACKED UP
Stephanie Nielson, contributing lifestyle editor for HOLIDAY, created a tree of sweets (opposite) by stacking cake stands and topping them with a paper tree, made by threading a flat-bottomed skewer through the center of paper flower ornaments of graduated sizes. She and her children filled the stands with yummy cupcakes, cookies, ornaments, and candy cups.

SMILE!
Claire, 11, shows off the candy wreath she made with her mother. Directions on page 44.

STARBURST TOPIARIES AND TREE TOPPERS

"These trees look great lining a mantle or along your dining table," Stephanie says. *Follow steps 1–8 to make them (or a stunning tree topper) by downloading the pattern from HolidayWithMatthewMead.com.*

You will need:

> Paper
> Scissors
> Pencil
> Ruler
> Circle templates (available on our website: HolidayWithMatthewMead.com)
> Wide rubber band, cut into two 1-inch pieces
> Needle and thread

1. Using our template as a guide, trace and cut out ten paper circles.

2. For each circle, use a ruler and pencil to divide it into eight equilateral triangles, and then cut along the lines toward the middle, stopping ½-inch from the center of each circle.

3. Wrap each "triangle" around the pencil, starting with a long side, to curl it into a cone, and secure with a dab of hot glue. Repeat for remaining circles until you have 10 star shapes.

4. Poke the needle and thread (knotted at the end), through the center of one of the rubber band pieces. Push the needle through the center points of five of the completed stars with their flat sides facing down. Turn over the remaining five stars, flat sides facing up, and thread them on, followed by the second piece of rubber band.

5. With the pencil, apply pressure to the rubber band to compress the stars into a ball and pull up on the string with your other hand to join the rubber pieces. Adjust the paper cones as needed to make the full three-dimensional starburst.

To make the topiaries:

6. Guide a white-painted dowel through the center of two ornaments, and secure as necessary with hot glue.

7. Press dowel into a painted flowerpot filled with floral foam.

8. Cover foam with small red candies.

"I love the idea of filling a hard-working, colorful tote with tree-trimming supplies"

— Stephanie, NieNieDialogues.blogspot.com

READY, SET, DECORATE!
The Nielsons' eldest son, Oliver, gathers up the newly crafted ornaments, including large dove stickers from a crafts store, to hang on the tree and to form into festive garlands.

"Inviting our children to help us deck the halls fills them with such excitement." — *Stephanie*

CUT AND PASTE

Three-dimensional paper ornaments are an inexpensive way to decorate your holiday home.

You will need:

    Templates
    Scissors
    Double-stick tape
    Hole punch
    Clear monofilament line

1. Download the templates from our website, HolidayWithMatthewMead.com, then use a computer to enlarge and print three of each pattern.

2. Cut out each flower or circle shape; fold each shape down its center.

3. Adhere three like shapes together using double-sided tape.

4. Using a hole punch, make a tiny hole at the top of each ornament and thread loops of clear monofilament line.

1

2

3

CANDY BY THE POUND

Look no further than your local sweets shop for inspiration for a multitude of festive projects and gifts. **1.** To make this candy wreath, paint a 6-inch wooden wreath form red, and then use crafts glue to stick an assortment of colorful candy to it. Stephanie used a mix of candied almonds, mints, raspberry marshmallows, and cinnamon candies. Attach a small picture hanger to the back and hang securely from a door or wall. **2.** Cellophane bags filled with candy become fun place cards or party favors when personalized with folded paper cardstock and alphabet stickers; staple along the cards to secure. **3.** Stephanie and the children fill clear glass or plastic ball ornaments (from a crafts store) with candy and use a ribbon to hang the fun decorations on their tree. **4.** Miniature cupcakes, covered in a thick layer of creamy white frosting, are sprinkled with crushed, striped peppermints. Decadent chocolate cookies (see recipe page 234) are nestled in cheery red muffin cups and studded with assorted red candies.

1

2 **3**

4

CANDY STATION

Create a festive display at one end of a room or along a wide hallway by stacking colorful benches and arranging jars of Christmas candy, collectibles, holiday treat bags, and handmade holiday décor on each level.
1. To make this simple wall tree (opposite) cut 80 circles out of patterned scrapbook paper using 2-inch circle punches. Arrange the circles and adhere using temporary glue dots, called Zots™. Set a cylindrical vase filled with tiny Christmas ornaments below the tree and hang the candy wreath (instructions on page 44) as a topper. **2.** Stephanie loves the innocent appeal of snowmen and created this 3-foot tall paper version using a variety of 12x12-inch scrapbook papers and heavy white paper. Trace a set of graduated bowls onto both the patterned and white papers. Use double-sided tape to adhere the circles together. Use wide-tip markers to draw on the snowman's face and buttons. Attach to a wall or door using Zots™. **3.** The Nielson children, including Oliver, 6, and Jane, 8, love it when their parents engage them in craft projects, especially during the holidays. **4.** Stephanie found these snowmen picks at a crafts store and tucks them into potted plants, flower arrangements, or uses them as gift toppers.

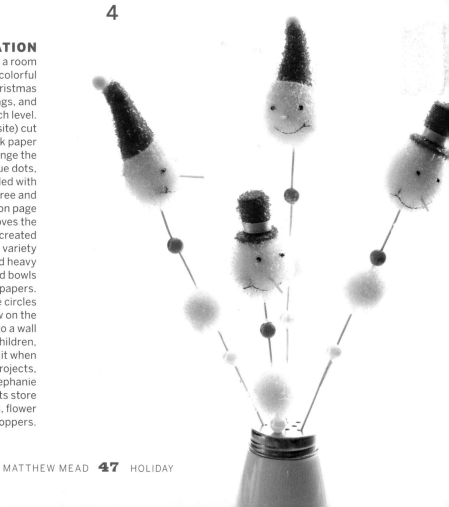

HOLIDAY COOKIES

Take back the ritual of "tea and cookies" by sampling some of our favorite recipes. Each cookie, when savored with a hot drink or some cold milk, is a gift you can give yourself.

PRETTY ENOUGH TO EAT

One of the best assets of these Iced Ginger Cookies (opposite) is their snap—or brittle, crispy consistency. If you can refrain from eating them all, they will stand up as edible ornaments and package decorations as well. Invite your children to help make them during an afternoon baking session.

SEAL AND SHIP

Bake an extra batch of cookies to share. Use collectible tins lined with tissue paper or a linen tea towel to transport the fragile treats (this page). Turn one cookie into a tag by printing a monogram, then affixing it to the cookie with extra royal icing. An icing snowflake, which you can buy where cake-decorating supplies are sold, decorates another thin tin of cookies.

A MIXED BAG Tried and true, each of our holiday cookie recipes is delightfully different. Some are made from simple, pure ingredients while others take a little more time and attention to detail in their delivery. The variety shown in these cookies (this page) makes them perfect for sharing at cookie swaps or to wrap up in packages for the neighbors. Fill a tin with holiday favorites—like Five-Spice Snails (which use Chinese five-spice powder), Bourbon Balls, Almond Financiers, and Cardamom-Black Pepper Trees with Juniper Icing (see recipe page 60)—and give the gift of comfort and joy all wrapped up in the form of a delicious cookie. Our cookie recipes begin on page 234.

"Enjoy the melding of flavors as you bite into a cookie. Allow it to fill you up with equal parts sugar and comfort." — *Matthew*

1 | 2

3 | 4

COOKIE BREAK Dunk these Triple Chocolate Almond Biscotti (opposite) in espresso and revel in the blend of bold and sweet. **THIS PAGE: 1.** Pair melt-in-your-mouth Jam Thumbprints with cold milk to temper the sweetness of the filling. **2.** Thought to look like little gold bricks, these cake-like Almond Financiers date back to the late 19th Century. **3.** Salty, sweet, and sinful, peanut fans will love the chewy-crunchy goodness of these Salty Peanut Bars. **4.** To make these no-bake Dulce de Leche Crispy-Rice-Cereal Treats, top the cereal bars with a smooth, creamy layer of store-bought dulce de leche sauce. Finish with a sprinkle of white nonpareils, dragées, and icing snowflakes from the cake-decorating aisle of the crafts store. Sticky, gooey, and sweet, they are sure to be a crowd pleaser.

SWEET SELECTION
Add new cookies to your baking line-up. THIS PAGE (clockwise, from top left): Angel Kiss Cookies (recipe page 60) are a heavenly mix of white chocolate, cream cheese, dried apricots, and butter. Chocolate Walnut Wheels require only basic pantry ingredients. Chocolate Thumbprints are filled with chocolate and vanilla-bean ganache. Chocolate-Dipped Peanut Butter Cookies are a nod to a deliciously classic union. Bourbon Balls (opposite) ship well, making them a perfect gift to pop in the mail. Recipes begin on page 234.

FLAVORFUL MIX Enjoy the fruits of your labor. **1.** Freshly chopped nuts and a smooth texture give these Austrian Chocolate Balls their pop-them-in-your-mouth appeal. **2.** Cranberry Florentines are crispy cookies if eaten the same day you bake them, but chewy after that. **3.** Kids will love the appeal (and taste!) of these Five-Spice Snails, made using Chinese five-spice powder—a combination of cinnamon, anise seed, star anise, ginger, and cloves. **4.** Maple-Nut Cookies taste delicious with a glass of warmed cider; each bite of the rich, maple-infused cookies delivers an unexpected blend of flavor and texture.
OPPOSITE: Mouth-watering Citrus Hazelnut Cookies are dipped in warm, melted chocolate after baking.

A
Camera Craft
Portrait

TEA TIME Pour a hot cup of tea or coffee and indulge your sweet tooth. **THIS PAGE** (clockwise, from top left): These Cranberry and Dark Chocolate-Chip Cookies are both gluten-free and scrumptious. Glazed in a thin layer of lemony icing, Lemon Drop Cookies have ricotta cheese and lemon zest for tangy sweetness. A spicy holiday favorite, Molasses Ginger Snaps pair deliciously with a fresh, sliced apple. Crumbly and buttery, Sandies are an old-fashioned favorite.
OPPOSITE: Chocolate Crackle-Top Cookies are rolled in powdered sugar before baking and crackle prettily upon cooling. Stack them on a pedestal dish and see how long they last. All cookie recipes begin on page 234.

CARDAMOM-BLACK PEPPER TREES WITH JUNIPER ICING

These cardamom-spiced cookies, which have the subtle, pleasant aroma of a fir tree, taste sweet and crisp and pair well with a cup of herbal tea. Recipe by Kate Wheeler at Savour-Fare.com

You will need:

> ¾ cup salted butter
>
> 1 cup sugar
>
> 1 large egg
>
> 2 cups flour
>
> ½ teaspoon baking powder
>
> ½ teaspoon salt
>
> 1 Tablespoon cardamom
>
> ½ teaspoon freshly ground black pepper

Preheat the oven to 375°

1. Using a stand mixer on high speed, cream the butter with the sugar until fluffy and pale. Add the egg and mix thoroughly. Switch to low speed and add the flour, baking powder, salt, cardamom, and pepper; continue beating until everything is incorporated. Divide the dough in two, form into two flat disks, wrap in plastic, and chill the dough overnight.

2. Roll the dough disks out to about ¼-inch thick. Using a tree-shaped cookie cutter, cut out the cookies and arrange them on a cookie sheet lined with a silicone mat. Bake the cookies until lightly golden, about 10 minutes, and let cool thoroughly before icing.

FOR THE ICING

You will need:

> ¾ cup half-and-half, divided
>
> 2 Tablespoons crushed dried juniper berries
>
> 1 pound confectioner's sugar
>
> Decorations, such as silver dragées and gold-luster dust

1. Heat the half-and-half with the juniper berries until they reach a low simmer, remove from heat, and let the mixture cool in the refrigerator overnight.

2. Strain out the berries, and combine with the remaining half-and-half and the sugar. Whisk together until a thick glaze forms. Brush the icing over the cookies, making sure to coat the sides as well as the tops. Let the icing harden.

3. To decorate, splatter royal icing (see recipes beginning on page 234) over the iced cookies, top with dragées, and, when the icing has become firm, brush the trees with edible gold luster dust.

ANGEL KISS COOKIES

Take these delectable cookies out of the oven while they are still soft and the edges are just slightly browned. Recipe by Laura Phelps.

You will need:

> 2 sticks butter
>
> 8 ounces cream cheese
>
> 2 cups granulated sugar
>
> 2 cups all-purpose flour
>
> 1 cup white chocolate chips
>
> 1 cup dried apricots, chopped

Preheat oven to 350°

1. In a large mixing bowl, beat together butter and cream cheese, using an electric mixer on high speed, until smooth. Add sugar and mix until fluffy. Slowly add in the flour. Stir in chocolate chips and apricots.

2. Use a teaspoon to drop dough onto an ungreased cookie sheet, placing them about 2 inches apart.

3. Bake for about 10 minutes, until the edges start to brown. The centers will still be soft, but they will set as the cookies cool on the baking sheet for 3 minutes. Transfer to wire racks to cool completely.

Makes 3 dozen cookies.

EVER GREENS

Easy-to-make decorations in a fresh and varied palette elevates green from its supporting role to starring color status.

APPLE OF YOUR EYE

To make this market-fresh wreath (opposite), visit the florist for greenery with shiny leaves, such as boxwood and pieris japonica. Cut snippets and use floral wire to tie small bouquets of about five stems each. Use more wire to cover an 18-inch grapevine wreath with the bouquets; see photo on page 70 for guidance. Snip the wires off the ends of green floral picks (this page) and use the wood skewers to attach granny smith and golden delicious apples to the wreath. Insert the ends of the picks into the fruit and then stick the tips of the picks into the wreath, rotating the apples to show stems or shiny cheeks.

COLOR SPLASH Think beyond the prescribed holiday green-and-red union, and try a monochromatic look that blends chartreuse, sour apple, and jade (above). Pearly tree ornaments and a gift box wrapped in graphic wallpaper add a festive touch. Give holiday foods a kiss of color, too. These shortbread cookies (opposite) are infused with green tea, which tints the batter slightly. The hue boost comes from food gels, which you can purchase in several shades. You'll find the cookie recipe at HolidayWithMatthewMead.com, and starting on page 234.

There's no rule that says you have to pair green with red for the holidays. Sticking to just one color simplifies decorating decisions and makes it easier to use what you already have.

GLIMPSES OF GREEN At-hand decorative items, such as flowerpots and ribbons, assume a holiday accent.
1. Vintage ornaments and a lady's feather headband deck a bird's nest. **2.** A ceramic pot overflowing with fern fronds gets into the spirit with a pinned-on holiday message. Add letters to ribbon using transfers from the crafts-store scrapbooking aisle and a burnishing tool. **3.** Petite glass vases hold candle votives and create ambient sparkle when grouped en masse. **4.** Satin ribbons in several tart shades can be used as gift wrappings, wreath ties, or tabletop swags.

THE POWER OF COLOR
Just about the only thing these disparate items have in common is color. The blend of bright hues draws together a mid-century vase, an Asian teapot, and a stack of vintage books into an artful array. The vase wears a necklace of opalescent ornaments, but the holiday mood comes primarily from the color statement. Set up an arrangement like this on your mantel or coffee table.

Re-imagining ordinary, everyday items can breathe new life into your holiday style.

EAT YOUR GREENS

Gifts and menu items can convey the color mood as well. Recycle bottles to fill with cook's favorites, such as balsamic vinegar or infused oil (opposite). Pop in new corks then crown with scraps of velvet. Shop thrift stores for lone goblets you can fill with cookies, spice rubs, or fragrant honey. Secure a piece of vellum across the top with gold twine. A decadent chocolate cake, glazed in ganache and topped with pistachios, rests temptingly on a fluted cake stand (this page). Look for the recipe at HolidayWithMatthewMead.com and page 234.

THE SPICE OF LIFE Variety is also the key to interesting holiday décor. **1.** Display a spectrum of hues in ceramic vessels (these are $2 to $5 flea-market finds). **2.** Hypericum berries pop against the holly leaves threaded into this birch-branch wreath. **3.** For dinner-party panache, hot-glue greens and a hydrangea bloom to a 5-inch grapevine wreath, and string it from a guest's chair. **4.** Check garden centers and crafts stores for blank wreath forms, or repurpose one from years past. Wire branches of arborvitae to a wire form as a frothy backdrop. **OPPOSITE:** Later, thread floral wire through limes and tie them on.

"Wreaths are a traditional sign of hospitality, but they can look modern and new." — *Matthew*

Using what you already have for one-color holiday décor squashes the need to acquire more stuff.

BEING GREEN When you are ready to add holiday cheer to your home, "shop" your rooms for anything green. Pull scarves from drawers, fruit from the refrigerator, flowerpots in from the patio, and dinnerware from kitchen cupboards. Assemble everything, and then see what new groupings make sense, using these ideas as inspiration. Melding old and new glassware with branches from backyard trees creates a pretty mantel arrangement (opposite). For a quick-and-easy centerpiece (this page), fill a large shallow bowl with fruit and leaves.

FRESH MATERIAL Holiday décor sprouts from live greenery arrangements. **1.** For this inventive wreath, put a few cut tendrils of ivy into a water pick, then tape it to the back of a letter "O" from an old sign. **2.** Ask the florist or grocer for branches of live bay leaves, which are aromatic additions. **3.** Wrap pretty ribbons around a couple of branches for a quick-and-easy centerpiece bouquet. **4.** Choose natural elements for their color, texture, and varying foliage shapes. Holly leaves are shiny ovals, while arborvitae is lacy, for example. Also included are hydrangea, pieris japonica, cedar, and boxwood.

LOOKING FOR ILLUMINATION
Cast a glow in the heart of a conversational grouping
with this candle centerpiece. Using hot glue, attach
tufts of fluffy reindeer moss to a twig wreath. In the
center of the wreath, place a plate and three 10- and
6-inch pillar candles. Take care to extinguish the
candles before they burn down close to the wreath.

DECORATE

My house isn't ready for Christmas until the final layers
are added: when evergreen garlands swag across
the doorways, and wreaths top the mantlepieces. Jenny
and I add candles and twinkle lights and lots of
potted mini trees and amaryllis bulbs. We fill bowls with
fragrant spices like cloves and cinnamon, and carefully
unwrap ornaments to hang on trees, from chandeliers,
and in windows. Christmas carols hum from our
stereo speakers as we unfurl a tree skirt and hang
stockings. It's always fun to feel the house come to life in
its most merry vestments. And when we are done,
we simply sit quietly in awe of the tree. No matter the date,
the season has not fully arrived until we decorate.

RED & WHITE DELIGHT

The bright colors of the season inspire a fanciful holiday gathering where the trimmings are sure to set creativity swirling.

IT'S A WRAP
An ironstone star box (opposite) makes a striking statement when set upon a collection of vintage Turkey red linens. An old arched storm window (this page), made merry by a coat of red paint, adds instant architecture to the room and offers a place for Matthew to hang paper ornaments made by his assistant, Lisa Smith-Renauld. He likes to wrap gifts here after the sun goes down, when the fading light prevents him from shooting projects in the studio.

VERY MERRY

Each year, Matthew decorates the studio and hosts a small breakfast gathering for a handful of his creative friends. Because the studio is a blank canvas, it is ideal for decorating on a whim. Recently, the Meads were delighted to host Paul and Lianne Stoddard, the artists and owners of Swirly Designs. This talented Massachusetts couple creates painted polymer clay ornaments for their online shop, SwirlyDesigns.com. Earlier in the season they gifted Matthew with whimsical snowman ornaments and cupcake picks—thus inspiring the cheery red and white color scheme. **OPPOSITE:** Paper petals are pinned to a straw wreath and hung from a chair. Use the petal pattern on page 248.

"Red and White is a happy color palette, and using it during the holidays reminds me to engage the colors year-round."

— Matthew

1

2

5

HOLIDAY BRUNCH

The Stoddards glean inspiration from their love of all things holiday and their glittery snowmen are made festive with jaunty red hats and collars. "The inspiration for the mini-snowmen wind-catchers (previous page) came from one of our children's parties. Intrigued by the movement of the paper streamers in the breeze, we decided to incorporate them into one of our designs," Lianne says. "Adding streamers to the snowmen brings that touch of whimsy that we love." As a nod to their creativity, Matthew paid close attention to the details of the breakfast buffet and focused on the décor for his talented guests: **1.** For a fun and decorative breakfast idea, stamp room-temperature hard-boiled eggs with holiday messages using simple letter stamps. **2.** Embroidered fabric hearts can hang from tree branches or cupboard doors. **3.** Jelly donuts, dusted with sugar, are delicious paired with a hot cup of coffee. **4.** A cut-paper dove is easily made with supplies from the crafts store, or download the template from HolidayWithMatthewMead.com. **5.** Handmade and charming, these holiday cards can be framed for a lasting, take-home keepsake. **6.** A pillow from Company C is a graphic inspiration. **7.** A mix of oats, honey, and dried fruits are offered in an apothecary jar and served with Greek yogurt.

3 4

6 7

HOLIDAY MESSAGE Decorating his studio to host a holiday breakfast is easy—Matthew's favorite props and collections are right at hand, and what he doesn't own, he simply makes! Matthew created this commemorative holiday print to share his seasonal wish to all. Resting on a shelf, it is a graphic backdrop to his red and white still-life vignette. To order a signed and numbered print (frame not included) visit HolidayWithMatthewMead.com; you can download the dove, heart, and star templates (opposite) there, or copy them on page 249.

MAKE IT Cut-paper ornaments hang from delicate branches coated with white spray paint and placed in a heavy vase.

GIFTS FROM NATURE

Step inside Matthew and Jenny's home as they usher in the holiday, embracing the natural beauty and snowy palette of the season.

ALL IS CALM
The living room is reflective of the pared-back elegance that the Meads are known for. Matthew fell in love with the consignment shop sofa and chair for their graceful lines and price ($350 for the pair). He re-upholstered both in painter's cloth and gave the frames a wash of gray paint. Simple greenery lends a festive note.

With a career filled with a heaping daily dose of colorful design and where the line between work and life often blurs, Matthew Mead strives for simplicity in his own home, especially during the holidays. As a collector of antiques and vintage treasures, it is, surprisingly, a pared-down style that truly defines his holiday décor. The festive season is one of Matthew's busiest times at the studio, and it doesn't allow for a lot of downtime. So, naturally, when Matthew and Jenny finally have a chance to tuck away at home for the week following Christmas, they revel in a peaceful, clean, and no-fuss environment. It is no coincidence that Matthew's holiday décor marries his love of nature—as seen in his first book, *Gifts From Nature* (Clarkson Potter, 1997)—with the clean, edited aesthetic found in his more recent book, *Entertaining Simple* (Wiley, 2007). To Matthew, holiday decorating has always been a way to embrace the season, and he aims for a wintry style that he can live with for several months. Both he and Jenny love that their quiet color palette allows their collections and the design of their furnishings to stand out—creating a relaxing environment for a holiday focused on spending time with family and friends.

FINE DETAILS Jenny's writing desk is the perfect spot to sit and address holiday cards. Her beloved collection of mercury glass rests there year-round and sparkles in the glow of the show-stopping light that Matthew created for her. A former Salvation Army cast-off, the lamp was transformed by removing the socket and rewiring it so the light illuminates from the round base. A boxwood wreath, hanging above, is an organic touch that Jenny doesn't rush to take down after the holiday. The couple uses natural, non-shedding greenery like lemon and laurel leaves (above right) to tuck into vases and pots throughout their home. OPPOSITE: Display collections in new ways. Place ornaments in bowls or arrange items in bookcases, in shadow boxes, or under glass domes. When Christmas passes, simply remove festive elements and add in fresh white flowers and wintry décor like sparkly glass snowflakes, simple glass votives, or snowball ornaments for enduring seasonal style.

FORM MEETS FUNCTION Matthew and Jenny always host Christmas dinner and every available chair is filled with family members and friends who are in town for the holidays. Known for his considerable culinary flair, Matthew likes the place settings and delicious food to take center stage on the table, so he keeps the table décor to a minimum. Favorite pieces from his ironstone collection make a statement when grouped together and he often puts several to use to hold cranberry sauce, chutney, and gravy. In the dining room window, Matthew hung a translucent quilt-patterned screen—a creative alternative to the more expected drapery.

ALL IS WHITE

In the dining room, Matthew pairs modern styling with sophisticated antiques and keeps the wall color, window treatments, and accessories monochromatic and graphic. For drama, they installed an ornate chandelier over a vintage metal Parsons table, and its shapely silhouette balances one of Matthew's favorite finds: a bench created from an early wood-lattice radiator cover. On the table, a collection of ironstone is grouped together for their differences in height and filled with holiday greens.

"As collectors, Jenny and I love that visitors to our home often remark that there is something beautiful to look at wherever they glance." — *Matthew*

THE ART OF THE COLLECTION The Meads enjoy creating studies throughout their home. Each vignette is edited, deliberate, and artfully arranged: **1.** Matthew counts fake snow as one of his guilty pleasures. He delights in how it makes everything look as though Jack Frost has danced about his home. **2.** A transferware platter bearing lemon leaves, stone spheres, and acorns adds natural holiday style. **3.** A terrarium is planted with mini-evergreens, which can be trimmed as they grow. **4.** Mercury glass adds sparkle and light. **5.** Jenny loves a natural, unadorned holiday tree, revelling in its simple beauty and form. Set atop an antique porcelain drinking fountain, it is a quiet nod to the holiday icon. **6.** Matthew crafted this wreath using paper medallions (patterns on page 252), first folding the medallions to add dimension and then gluing them to a wire wreath form. **OPPOSITE:** An old glass pie case showcases a collection of pierced silverplate.

MERRY LITTLE COTTAGE

Combine a pretty mix of vintage floral finds, fresh greens, and fragrant roses with some colorful cottage charm to add a dash of merry to this romantic Christmas in the country.

ROSY WELCOME
A rich evergreen wreath (opposite) provides
the perfect backdrop for overblown English
roses. To make, place each rose clipping into
a water pick and use floral wire to attach the
blooms to the wreath; hang indoors. Sprinkle
a dusting of faux snow onto roses in a natural
grouping (this page) for a frosty flourish.

PRETTY LITTLE DETAILS Let nature guide the décor: **1.** Place fresh roses in water picks and invite children to help trim the tree. **2.** Choose roses in shades of burgundy, soft pink, and cerise for a soft palette. **3.** Vintage hydrangea blossoms adhered to a foam ball offer a botanical nod to the traditional Christmas ornament. **4.** A floral plate is a fresh and unexpected place setting for Christmas dinner. **OPPOSITE:** A jauntily painted farmhouse table holds a copper-lined tray filled with vintage floral ceramics and pink mercury glass ornaments. An eclectic mix of flea market chairs offers up casual seating for a nourishing break from holiday chores, complete with freshly baked treats.

FANCY FLORALS Be on the hunt for floral ephemera. Antique papers and fabrics inspire graphic wall treatments and special floral gift wraps. Look for old ribbons and trims to dress up packages, homemade stockings, and evergreen wreaths.

RECLAIMED ART
Color-copy vintage wallpaper scraps for gift wrap and tags, and to create a temporary wall treatment (opposite). A lamp with a damaged shade needs no embellishment when placed in front of a backdrop of vintage graphic prints and bowls filled with shimmery garland and pink glass ornaments.

SWEET GIFTS Specialty cupcakes (this page) are a pretty departure from cookies. Colorful fondants and icings transform the little cakes into unexpected presents, and it only takes one to surprise almost anyone on your gift list. Red velvet cupcakes (opposite) need little embellishment, achieving festive status from their rich, red color. Vintage coasters add a sweetly romantic touch to their otherwise simple presentation.

Gather floral finds all year long and bring them out at the holidays for a delightfully romantic and unexpected holiday theme.

DECK THE HALLS Floral fabrics in shades of pink and blue pair well with vintage ornaments, and fresh roses can be found readily. Assemble natural elements, such as these greens, wreaths, and pinecones (opposite), with pretty packages to welcome guests. A floral notions holder (this page) organizes cards, candles, and gift tags and keeps them within easy reach. Tuck in some greenery and ornaments. To make a charming advent calendar, use a pattern and floral fabric and slip some surprises into each pocket to mark the countdown to Christmas.

GET THE LOOK

A wire topiary form, sans vines, takes center stage when bedecked with vintage ornaments.

Gather ornaments from tag sales and second-hand stores. Hand-painted and glittered ones hold special appeal.

Use floral fabric remnants to dress up the back of a chair or to drape a table. Small swatches can be made into evergreen sachets for gifts.

Antique cache pots and urns can be filled with roses in varying shades and degrees of bloom.

Gather floral dishes and ceramic pieces and fill them with ornaments, greens, and fresh flowers.

THE DECORATED TREE

With a vast collection of ornaments to inspire him and nature to set an example, designer Darryl Moland shares his talents for festooning our favorite symbol of the holiday.

PHOTOS BY DARRYL MOLAND AND HAROLD DANIELS

SNOWY DELIGHTS

Dripping with glass and silver icicles, these trees are tiny versions of the giant hemlocks Darryl Moland encountered in a mountain forest on Christmas morning in 2010. He photographed the trees, crusted in snow and sparkling in the sunshine, so he could recreate their glitter with ornaments he has collected over the years. A beaded Czechoslovakian star crowns this silvery tinsel tree, but most of the ornaments came from mail order and import stores stateside. A white base (opposite) mimics the snow bank that might blow up around the base of a tree.

WINTER WISH

DARRYL MOLAND'S PASSION for decorating Christmas trees sprouted early—very early. "I was about 9 or 10 when my mother let me decorate the family's tree for the first time," Darryl says. As he writes in his recently published book, *The Decorated Tree* (2011; Blurb.com), it was never a chore: "I would lose myself in all the lights and glitter."

Those early trees were familiar to us all: meaningful family ornaments sharing prickly branches with metallic garland and blinking colored bulbs. But as the seasons passed, Darryl's vision for a different, more natural holiday tree emerged. "I started making wreaths and garlands from fresh greenery after the plastic varieties came into popular use," he writes. One Christmas, he urged his family to buy a live white pine with its root ball intact, and after the holiday they planted it in the front yard. Each year, despite his Southern climate's stingy allotment of snow, he studied the tree and thought of ways to festoon it.

Today, a snow-capped hemlock spied on a walk through the north Georgia woods is just as likely to inspire him. As the creative force behind TheDecoratedTree.blogspot.com, which showcases a different seasonal tree every month for holidays as varied as Mother's Day and winter solstice, Darryl looks everywhere for ideas. "I want my trees to have some meaning or relevance to the natural world," he says. Gone are the colored bulbs. In fact, there are no lights at all. He twists and twines branches of small, wire trees until they look natural, and lades them with a fascinating array of ornaments. He's likely to blend a beaded Czechoslovakian star with a vintage Gorham sterling silver icicle and new mercury glass bird from Target—as long as the overall look conveys meaning or evokes a memory. "I'm trying to tell a story with my trees," he says.

WINTER WONDERLAND Take cues from nature to decorate your tree. **1.** Darryl compiled his popular blog entries into a coffee table book available through Blurb.com (blurb.com/bookstore/detail/2804026). **2.** In December 2010, Darryl delighted in a rare snowfall in Georgia. "I was like a little kid," he says of the Christmas morning treat. Photo by Jon Chavez. **3.** A beaded tree topper has icy sparkle. **4.** Darryl photographs scenes in hopes of inspiring future decorated trees. **5.** Darryl tries to stage a scene, rather than just decorate a tree. Wrapped gifts and a glitter-covered reindeer around the tree base reinforce the colors and theme. **6.** When not in use, Darryl's ornament and figurine collection resides in dozens of tissue-paper-filled boxes. "I rent a storage space," he admits.

THE BEST MODEL With photographs of live trees on his camera's memory card or on the vintage postcards he gathers, Darryl has no shortage of scenes to emulate. This adolescent maple inspired a spare tabletop homage (right), which started with a paper-wrapped wire twig by David Stark. Darryl anchored it in an aluminum vase, which he antiqued and filled with faux snow. Scandinavian folded paper stars and German lametta tinsel icicles add sparkle, while the snowy color comes from white paper leaves and ornaments that look like vintage milk glass.

THROUGH THE WOODS Decorate a tree to conjure memories. **1.** Snow globes are stacked on journals where Darryl jots his ideas. **2.** A briefly blanketed branch is preserved. **3.** As someone who has never lived farther north than Atlanta, Darryl doesn't take images like this snow-shadowed log for granted. **4.** A stand of trees pose for his camera. **OPPOSITE:** Woodland critters take part in a scene erected on a candle stand. Easy to store and quick to set up, small trees let Darryl decorate several during one season. And he doesn't just stick to December: This tree may reappear as a June bridal tree.

"I think the holiday tree should celebrate the seasons, whether with color, texture, or ornaments that evoke the natural world." —Darryl Moland

ALL BOXED UP

The faded colors and muted tones of well-loved ornaments and timeworn fabrics recall the charm of Christmases gone by. Look to vintage collectibles and distressed furniture to create an unforgettable holiday scene. Recycled floral boxes can be used to package gifts like handmade ornaments and vintage tea cups—with no gift wrap needed. Simply finish with an organza ribbon and top with a tiny holiday ornament.

TIMEWORN TIDINGS

Add a vintage patina to your holiday decorating with faded florals, soft pastels, and simple projects that stand the test of time.

PAPER ROSES WREATH

Pastel tissue-paper flowers form a dazzling wreath.

You will need:

- 12-inch foam wreath form
- 6x6-inch tissue paper squares in pastel hues
- Floral wire

1. To make flowers, accordion-fold five stacked layers of tissue paper. Wrap floral wire around the middle of the folded tissue and secure. Create different petals by snipping each end of the paper folds in a pointed or rounded shape. Fan out each half of the folds on one side, up towards the middle; repeat for the other side. Separate and fluff all of the tissue layers to form a flower shape. Make about 30 flowers.

2. Hot-glue the flowers to cover the wreath form.

3. Attach tiny mercury balls with additional floral wire.

TRIM THE TREE Vintage glass ornaments and paper fans dress a white tree (THIS PAGE). To make a fan, use a 12x12-inch piece of scrapbook paper and make ½-inch wide accordion folds. Once entirely pleated, fold in half and tape together using double-sided tape, then fan out the pleats. For smaller fans, use smaller sheets of scrapbook paper. For interest, layer small fans on top of large ones and adhere using hot glue. Nestle the fans in the tree branches.

HUNG WITH CARE Retro balls and faux birds (OPPOSITE) are hallmarks of vintage holiday style. Pastel tissue-paper flowers add soft color, and balance the bold hues of the glass balls.

COLORFUL COLLECTIONS Dig through your grandmother's attic or scour flea markets for vintage decorations. **1.** Collect glass ornaments in your favorite colors and bring back the memories of childhood holidays. **2.** Create quiet impact by focusing your tree décor on a theme. Here, we chose a nostalgic mix of vintage and shiny—unified by a palette of pink, peach, and blue. **3.** Place leftover ornaments on a scalloped antique platter. We made the sparkly bird's nest using a short length of silvery tinsel. **4.** Make an accordion-pleated tree skirt using pretty patterned gift wrap. To make, follow the fan directions on page 116.

OLD STYLE
The tiered wooden stand and fret-work bird ornament are from Matthew's new home accessories collection. To buy, visit Etsy.com/Shop/MatthewMeadVintage.

OLD-FASHIONED FAVORS Small glass bottles, filled with pearlescent gum balls, are a delightful take-home treat. Wrap tinsel around the neck of each bottle and tie on a miniature vintage mercury glass ornament.

IN BLOOM Fill several large glass jars with water and add in small bouquets of lush pink and orange roses (OPPOSITE) for a breathtaking and unexpected holiday centerpiece. Set into a large wire mesh basket for easy portability throughout your home, or use bouquets for sweet last-minute gifts when friends or neighbors pop in for an unexpected holiday visit.

QUICK IDEAS **1.** Break with tradition and fill a pillowcase with small gifts and finish with a pretty ribbon. **2.** Purchase a floral-patterned rectangular box at your local craft store. Enhance the design using colored pencils. **3.** Age an inexpensive journal from a bargain shop by white-washing the cover. Apply white stain with a paint brush and let set for one minute. Wipe off excess stain until desired effect is achieved. Tie a ribbon around the journal and embellish with a pretty pencil and a small ornament. **4.** Decorate gifts with sugar-paste flowers purchased from your local craft or bakery shop.

WALL SACHETS
Cover plain hanging sachets with scrapbook paper, trims, and stickers.

CHRISTMAS PRESENT

Executive Editor Linda MacDonald opens the doors of her holiday home to share her approach to celebrating simply.

DECK THE HALLS

Tradition abounds in a home filled with family, simple celebrations, and a freshly modern take on all things pretty. In the entry, a vintage inspired silver tree (opposite) is hung with a complimentary palette of ornaments. The theme is changed yearly with a rotation of treasured ornaments, many of which are vintage.

IN OUR HOUSE, holiday traditions are as important as the people from whom they pass down. We embrace the traditions that enhance our holiday and discard the rest. Having emigrated as a child from Northern Ireland to Canada, I still cling to some of our early traditions like Christmas crackers, trifle, and clothes-pinning a sock to the foot of our beds to be filled with juicy oranges and Cadbury Flakes. Yet as entrenched as I get in holiday planning and decorating, I bristle at the notion of defining Christmas as "work." While our family naturally gets caught up in the bustle of the season, we strive to simplify what we can, including gift-giving, entertaining, and cooking. In essence, we avoid the temptation to amp things up socially, and instead prefer to gather close friends and family for glittery craft sessions, bake not-so-perfect cookies, and cheat by hosting after-dinner dessert parties. When decorating for the holidays I stay true to the color palette in our home: cool watery blues, grey-greens, warm creams and whites, punctuated by hits of citrusy yellow. Happily, it has resulted in a seasonal palette that works with our snowy winters and reminds me that no matter how far I have travelled to settle into my Nova Scotia home, it is family and the memories and traditions of my heritage that truly make me feel at home.

COMFORT AND JOY Our living room (opposite) is our home's year-round gathering place for friends and family, including our children Grayson, Callum, and Sophie. A comfy and casual space, nothing is placed in there that is too precious to be used and enjoyed, and slipcovers and washable pillow cases are staples. Although it's a hard-working room, I still want it to be pretty, so ruffled pillows and shades of chartreuse add girly charm. On a restless whim one day, I wallpapered an area above the sofa to add interest. My husband Paul framed it in an hour and has, in fact, made most of the furniture in our home. SOURCES: lamp, pillows: Homesense; rug: Company C. Vintage glassware (above left) is brought out on special occasions only. Cousins Sarah, Sophie, and Ella (above right) love to get together during the holidays and their giggles can be heard throughout the house.

1 2

3

4

6

5

JUST DESSERTS

My contemporary light fixture from IKEA makes a bold statement in the dining area (opposite). Its largesse adds an element of surprise and boasts an ethereal, seasonal appeal—conjuring up images of a large dandelion puff in the warmer months and of a giant snowball in winter. On the table, an array of baked sweets adds up to an oh-so-popular dessert party.

HOLIDAY FLAIR

While I could never be accused of being a decorating minimalist, I do find myself paring back a bit and allowing our favorites to take center stage: simple hurricanes filled with favorite ornaments, a family room tree devoted to our collection of *A Christmas Story* ornaments (our favorite holiday movie), and shadow boxes bearing little snowy scenes we create ourselves. Adding a festive note to our home is a special part of my holiday.

1. My mother, Jane, and I have a yearly tradition of crafting with a little glitter, fabric, and our trusty glue guns; Sophie joins us and we find glitter on the floor for days.
2. Gingerbread cookies don't last long when dusted in powdered sugar.
3. Watery blues are carried through into my kitchen where nods to vintage style exist throughout. Our cabinets are painted in a soft blue-grey and I love scouring thrift shops for retro-modern dishes and serving pieces. Paul made the kitchen island for our tenth anniversary and he designed it with an old-fashioned candy counter in mind.
4. Callum, 16, reaches for his favorite—pecan tarts served with a dollop of fresh cream.
5. My mantel is deep, so I prefer to showcase larger items for impact or group small collectibles on a large platter or in a substantial glass vessel. I secure glass ball ornaments to a favorite tray using Zots™.
6. Sophie and I are "Team Holiday" in our home, taking the most pleasure in decorating, baking and crafting while the boys sit back and reap the rewards!

CHRISTMAS
HOLIDAY
YULETIDE
SEASONS
GREETINGS
SILENT NIGHT
NOEL
TWELVE DAYS
MERRY AND
BRIGHT
JINGLE BELLS

COOL TIDINGS Quiet little spots like this (opposite), with just a few collectibles and meaningful objects, are restful to the eye. Matthew made this holiday "subway" sign for me as a Christmas gift. You can purchase one like it via our website, HolidayWithMatthewMead.com. In spirit with the rest of the house, the focus of our master bedroom (above) is cool color and frilly textures. Paul made the bed—naturally! SOURCES: Bedding, Pinecone Hill (PineConeHill.com). Lamps and accent cushions: Homesense.

1　**2**

3　**4**

VISIONS OF SUGARPLUMS Trifle is my favorite dessert, and my mother makes it for me every Christmas. (Find Linda's Mum's Trifle on our recipe pages, beginning page 234). **2.** Our eldest son Grayson, 18, can finally be trusted to serve dessert and not steal a swipe at the icing. **3.** Sophie, 11, shows her father the path Santa might travel to get to our house. **4.** Dip cake bites, made with cake and cream cheese frosting, in candy coating and drizzle with icing for a child-sized treat kids will love. Even simpler? Dip doughnut holes into the coating for a similar effect. **OPPOSITE:** Petite cakes, dusted in icing sugar, await slicing.

BLUE CHRISTMAS

Holiday decorating need not be expensive or difficult. A scarf hanger (opposite) from IKEA is re-imagined as impromptu frames for favorite ornaments, gift tags, and paper crafts. SOURCES: Fawn and bird tags and cards, Vintage Paper Parade (Etsy.com/Shop/VintagePaperParade). THIS PAGE: I wrote most of my stories for HOLIDAY sitting at this little desk that Paul made me.

NATURAL HOLIDAY

Take advantage of the season's bounty—a fragrant supply of spices, berries, and fresh greens—to create easy decorating projects that will infuse your house with homespun warmth.

CORNUCOPIA OF IDEAS This time of year, it's a cinch to gather up natural offerings that are plentiful in the grocery store, and maybe even your own back yard. Pine trees shed their cones, the cranberry harvest hits the produce aisle, and ingredients for potpourri or mulled cider are set out in bulk bins. Dig in and fill your basket. Whether you just array items in a wooden platter (this page), or spend an afternoon fashioning them into fetching tree decorations (opposite), these presents from nature enhance your home with a feeling of timeless simplicity.

1. LIGHT THE WAY

Not only are these items pretty in their unrefined way, but they give off aromas that many of us associate with happy holiday memories. Set a small votive candle in a glass container (Matthew chose one of his favorite vintage jelly jars; available at Etsy. com/Shop/MatthewMeadVintage), and tuck fresh cranberries around it. The warmth from the candle will encourage some of the berry fragrance. Nearby, a sprig of bay leaf also has a crisp scent. Sprinkle clippings or the individual leaves between candles down the center of the table for an irresistible combination. And remember, never leave a burning candle unattended; burnt cranberries don't smell nearly as good as gently warmed ones.

2. HANGING AROUND

These rustic wreaths capture the appeal of a nature walk and are easy to make. For the pinecone circles, cut wreath forms out of cardboard. These measure 5 and 7 inches in diameter. Wrap the cardboard in brown ribbon and secure the ends with hot glue. Rub the tines off several pinecones, then use hot glue to attach then in overlapping layers to cover the ribbon. When finished and dry, make the tines shine with a dusting of gold embossing powder. For the twig wreath, wrap brown twine around the junctions of four pairs of straight, fresh cut branches. You can also purchase similar wreaths already made from crafts stores. Adorn the wreath with a cluster of dried embellishment, such as whole star anise, allspice berries, and other floral supplies from the craft store.

3. MIXED MEDLEY

Stir up your own batch of potpourri to use around the house or to give away. In a large mixing bowl, combine a variety of scented and natural ingredients. We used things we picked up on a walk, such as small pinecones, acorns, and horse chestnuts. Then we embellished the mix with purchased ingredients, including almonds and pecans in their shells, fresh bay leaves, whole star anise, cinnamon sticks, rose hips, and birch bark curls. When you have about 8 cups of ingredients in the bowl, stir in ½ cup of orris root powder, which we bought from an online spice store. It has a faint violet scent and is often used as a preservative in potpourri. We also stirred in 2 ounces of bayberry oil, but you can choose any essential oil you find appealing.

4. WEE WREATH

Use the same technique as the larger wall wreaths to fashion this napkin ring. Cut a small circle form from heavy-duty cardboard (Matthew sacrificed an extra box for these projects); this one measures 2½ inches in diameter. Hot-glue small pinecone tines around the circle and add whole star anise to the top. Gold embossing powder adds extra shine. Nestle the ring into a complementary table setting, including a hardy linen napkin, chunky pottery dinnerware, unpolished silver flatware, and a textural table runner. This runner is part of Matthew's collection of antique linens, but a reproduction of it (and the jelly jar candleholder) is available for sale at Etsy.com/ Shop/MatthewMeadVintage.

HUNTING AND GATHERING HELP

You can gather handfuls of acorns, pinecones, and fallen leaves on public land near your home. But if you need large quantities of clean, unblemished materials, it's best to go to a retail source:

Knud Nielsen
KnudNielsen.com;
(800) 633-1682

Nature's Pressed Flowers
NaturesPressed.Com;
(800) 850-2499

Attar Herbs and Spices
AttarHerbs.com;
(800) 541-6900

1

2

3

4

HAVE A BALL Simple and organic, these eye-catching balls (this page) show off the textures and colors of nature. You can purchase similar novelties at stores that sell home accessories, fabric, and crafts. You can also make them by hot-gluing potpourri ingredients, cording, strings of beads, and wooden berries to the surface of plain foam crafts-store balls. When you have a selection, pile the balls into a galvanized-metal bucket.

RUSTIC VIEW Think inside the box to display some woodland finds (opposite). This flat, wide wreath form in a modern square shape is a friendly surface to adhere bumpy pinecones. Look for similar forms, usually made of twigs, at the crafts store. You can also purchase variety packs of pinecones, or gather different-size specimens during a walk through the woods. Heat up your glue gun and keep the refills coming as you attach enough cones to cover the frame. When finished, tuck dried moss from the garden center or crafts store into any gaps.

"I am so grateful for the gifts Mother Nature sends."
— Matthew

1. PRETTY LITTLE PACKAGES

These small containers are an elegant way to show your gratitude. Tuck a small trinket, gift card, or movie passes inside a vintage cold cream jar, or set up a wee terrarium that brings holiday cheer. For the tabletop garden, arrange reindeer moss, cranberries, and ivy sprigs in a glass compote or lidded candy jar. Another gift idea uses sleek silver tins from the office supply store: Fill them with writing supplies, including a fountain pen, address labels, and stamps. Bind the boxes together with a ribbon, and add a sprig of greenery.

2. NO-SEW STOCKING

With scissors and glue, you can whip up this cheery stocking in any size you like. Download the stocking template from HolidayWithMatthewMead.com, enlarge it to your desired size, and then trace it twice onto a piece of felt. Join the two stockings, using fabric glue around the edges. To make the cuff, first color-copy the leaves onto iron-on printer fabric, which is sheets of 8x10-inch fabric designed to work with home printers. (Look for it at crafts and fabric stores.) Print the leaves, cut them out, and iron them onto the stocking, following the manufacturer's directions. Finally, glue on artificial cranberries.

3. FRAME UPS

Create festive and personal ornaments by choosing the elements you want to feature, such as pressed leaves and pretty papers, or computer-printed sayings, carol titles, or quotes. Then have several pairs of inexpensive glass pieces cut at a local hardware store. Ours measure 2½x3½ inches and 4x4 inches. Sandwich the papers between two pieces of glass, and bind the edges with 1-inch-wide copper tape, which you can buy at home centers, crafts stores, and online. As a final touch, affix copper wire hangers with more glue.

LEAF PRESSING

Any kind of tree foliage—from these red maple leaves, to oak, birch, or laurel leaves—can be pressed flat and dried. Simply place them between the pages of an old phone book, and weigh it down with a heavy rock or brick. Check the leaves every few days; it will take about a week for them to dry completely.

"Look deep into nature, and then you will understand everything better." —*Albert Einstein*

MIDWEST MERRIMENT

When three creative style entrepreneurs get together to enjoy some girl time, they can't help but deck the halls. Along the way, they share ideas and lots of laughs.

GIRL POWER Coffee kick-starts the day. **1.** Amy Barickman, Carol Spinski, and Debbie Dusenberry became friends as their Kansas City–based style businesses overlapped. They met at Carol's home for breakfast and a decorating blitz. **2.** The chandelier hosts vintage ornaments. **3.** Settling on a coral-and-chocolate palette beforehand, the gals brought accessories that would meld in the neutral interiors. Debbie's vintage doll umbrella is a tabletop bowl. **4.** Airy macaroons are tempting nibbles. **OPPOSITE:** Debbie brought the entry tree. Wrapped completely in white yarn ("I sat in front of the TV every night with hot glue," Debbie says), it elegantly displays ornaments. Debbie's bichon frise, Pearl, is a fan, and so is Carol: "It is un-real," she says admiringly.

"We get together
and bounce ideas
off each other—
everything from
business, to styling,
to publishing. It's
nice to have people
in your life who get
you and get what
you do." — *Carol Spinski*

STANDING TALL Debbie thought the paper feather tree (this page) would make a great centerpiece when the gals finished embellishing it. They sprayed it with coral-color crafts paint, and when it dried, strung it with collections of vintage and new ornaments and paper cutouts. Decorative packages (opposite) are tied up in chocolate-color ribbons. Mixing in brown and gold made the coral hue feel grown-up, Debbie says. "None of us is really into things that look too sweet or cute," she says.

1 2 3 4

FRIENDSHIP BENEFITS Friends can offer fresh perspectives on your holiday style. **1.** The aroma of a fruit tart wafted through the house while Amy, Carol, and Debbie worked. **2.** Carol usually lays frameless mirrors down the center of her farm table, but Debbie suggested propping them on the mantel to dazzling effect. **3.** The friends used one of Amy's pattern books to cut felt stars for the tree. **4.** Fir branches snipped from backyard trees provide fresh scent. **OPPOSITE:** The kitchen in Carol's rehabbed farmhouse illustrates her rustic-romantic style. "With a little French country added in—if that makes sense," she says with a laugh.

1   **2**

CREATIVITY UNLEASHED

After a career as a hospital nurse, Carol's creative spirit has emerged. In 2005, she and two friends opened Raised in Cotton (RaisedInCotton.com), a home furnishings and antiques shop in Raymore, Missouri. It has been wildly popular, and it has opened up all sorts of new opportunities, she says. Now also a photographer and event styler, she decorated the 1865 farmhouse (opposite) she shares with her husband.

3   **4**

A COLLECTOR'S HOME

1. Arrayed on a chest in front of the window, Carol's antique bottlebrush trees are all ivory. Even at Christmas, she keeps to the serene, tone-on-tone palette she prefers in her home.

2. Since this is a busy time of year in her store, Carol appreciates her friends helping make the house look merry for get-togethers she'll have with friends and family. Her three grown children, who live in the Kansas City area, will gather here. "It's really fun to do a big long farm table for everyone," she says. "I cut pine tree branches from the yard so I can mix in natural elements with my vintage stuff."

3. Carol dressed vintage apothecary bottles for the special occasion. She used double-sided tape to affix belts of lace that are pinned with rhinestone broaches and buttons.

4. Beaded snowflake ornaments will soon hang from tree branches or in front of frosted windowpanes.

5. To show off special ornaments, such as this hand-painted ball, Carol puts her mercury glass candlesticks to use as pedestals.

6. A vintage candy tin fits the coral color scheme.

5

6

CONJURING MEMORIES Handmade embellishments add nostalgic charm. **1.** Wee stockings with tatted lace cuffs hang from whitewashed branches. **2.** Amy Barickman of AmyBarickman.com is one of the country's experts on needle arts, and she has a company that publishes craft and sewing books. The handcrafted ornaments she brought to Carol's house are from a series of Marilyn Gash designs; you can order them at IndygoJunction.com. **3.** Felt stars are used as package adornments. **4.** Doves nested in a vintage bowl feature wings made of snippets of antique lace and crochet doilies. **OPPOSITE:** This vignette of timeworn books, crystalline faux snow, and detailed ornaments on one of Carol's coffee tables conveys the coziness of the season.

"Each of us brought our own treasures, and then it was a collaboration to help them find their places in the décor. It's great to have a friend's new perspective." — *Amy Barickman*

BRIGHT FUTURE

With a background in makeup artistry and movie production, Debbie Dusenberry is no stranger to reinvention. Recently, she transitioned her renowned Kansas City shop into an online business, CuriousSofa.com. The new format lets her change inventory with the whimsies of the seasons. Many of the items she brought to Carol's house, in fact, might be this year's holiday offerings.

COLLECTIVE INSPIRATION

1. A wicker reindeer basket hangs from one of Carol's many cupboards. She prefers the unfitted armoires to the too-perfect look of built-in cabinets, even limiting them in her kitchen. "I store all my dishes in them. I like things in their original, weathered finish," she says.

2. Though the patinaed silver punch bowl is Carol's, Debbie arranged the items inside. "It's filled with mercury glass, metal, and silver things. I love to do tone-on-tone arrangements," she says. Aware of the differences in their styles—Amy is more nostalgic; Carol likes primitive country looks; Debbie has a slight urban edge—Amy says the friends have so much in common. "We are drawn to a similar aesthetic and are focused on vintage materials and content," she says, which made developing a singular holiday look easy and fun. "We all love flea markets and antiques shows," Debbie says. "We all have great collections."

3. Sparkly glittered keys and a velvet-covered reindeer have the look of old-world trinkets.

4. Even though it doesn't tell time, this new ornament has the allure of a vintage cuckoo clock.

5. Fashion from eras gone by can have a decorative effect. This lady's sweater, with ornate beading and embroidery, hints at special occasions and festive events. Shop for special pieces at thrift stores and consignment shops, then display them on ribbon-wrapped hangers.

6. In the cupboard that Carol uses as a store-all for accessories and supplies, a metal office bin holds an assortment of ornaments.

GOLD RUSH

Give your home the Midas touch this season with a gilding that comes from Matthew's favorite precious metal. Follow his lead to create an upscale country look using paint, trimmings, and flea market finds.

1

2

3

4

5

6

7

8

GOLD STANDARD

Flea-market finds are reborn. **1.** A wreath of millinery flowers gets a misting of antique-gold floral spray. **2.** The cover of this vintage book looks the part. **3.** A fretwork bird gleams with a coat of liquid gold leaf. **4.** To incorporate the metal deer trophy, I painted it gray and festooned it with greens and garland. **5.** Painted and embellished with grapes, this salvaged architectural detail becomes a wreath. **6.** I printed a message, then inserted it into this old gold medallion. **7.** Bring in your favorite outdoor pieces, such as this worn gray statue, which have the patina to suit this style. **8.** This year, Jenny strung gold-bead garland to hang from trees, chandeliers, and doorframes. **OPPOSITE:** A gilded mirror crowns a vintage chair that I painted gray and antiqued with a brown glaze.

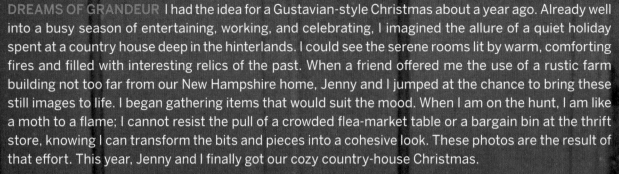

DREAMS OF GRANDEUR I had the idea for a Gustavian-style Christmas about a year ago. Already well into a busy season of entertaining, working, and celebrating, I imagined the allure of a quiet holiday spent at a country house deep in the hinterlands. I could see the serene rooms lit by warm, comforting fires and filled with interesting relics of the past. When a friend offered me the use of a rustic farm building not too far from our New Hampshire home, Jenny and I jumped at the chance to bring these still images to life. I began gathering items that would suit the mood. When I am on the hunt, I am like a moth to a flame; I cannot resist the pull of a crowded flea-market table or a bargain bin at the thrift store, knowing I can transform the bits and pieces into a cohesive look. These photos are the result of that effort. This year, Jenny and I finally got our cozy country-house Christmas.

GOLD LEAF
In this urn, sprigs of boxwood and dusty miller are natural foils for the bright pops of gold-painted magnolia leaves and seedpods I buy at the crafts store. At flea markets and estate sales during the year, I gather bits and pieces—postcards, coins, pocket-watch cases, and other metal findings—to use as gift tags and package embellishments (opposite).

GILT TRIP To weave the golden palette throughout the house, I perch vintage and new items on tabletops and shelves. Jenny sketched a tree on an old piece of slate (this page), and I used it as a backdrop for a vignette that includes a roll of twine, a silver tray, and faux snow. Elsewhere, I stacked wrapped gifts (opposite). Brushed with gold paint, wood emblems from the woodworking section of the crafts store make pretty package embellishments.

PRECIOUS METALS You can be flexible with a country house look. I enjoy mixing pieces from different centuries, for example, teaming something early with something modern. **1.** Gilded mirrors with interesting deteriorated finishes are easy to find at secondhand stores. **2.** A glint of gold is all that I needed to unite a mid-century compote with modern-day import store etched spheres. **3.** Candles are essential to the cozy environment. This metal votive candleholder casts a lacey shadow. **4.** I plucked some gold balls from my collection of mercury glass ornaments. **OPPOSITE:** This bookcase shows off items that create the look—vintage books, metal urns, and stone pieces with the patina of age.

LET IT SHINE Adding elements of gold give shine to even the most utilitarian objects. Galvanized watering cans (this page) are re-cast as Christmas stockings filled with gold-paper-wrapped gifts, candies, and cookies. At the entry to the farm building (opposite), fragrant forest greenery, touches of gold, and wrapped packages welcome our guests and hint that they are about to be transported to an Old World holiday.

CHRISTMAS ON THE CAPE

Cape Cod shop owner Lee Repetto welcomes you into her holiday home, expertly decorated in her unique brand of authentic nautical style.

ALL THE TRIMMINGS
Lee's guests appreciate her careful attention to detail, like the tiny gifts as table favors and the small German glass ornaments that she nestles in vintage glass goblets from a New Hampshire antiques shop.

HOLIDAY DINING
The table is set with old family dishes and new green plates from Lee's shop, The Spotted Cod. A striped rug from Dash and Albert and vintage pilasters, flanking a display niche, reflect Lee's ability to pair old with new.

ALL THROUGH THE HOUSE In the family room (opposite), a full height Christmas tree is trimmed with a garland of blue fish netting from Nova Scotia and a mix of treasured ornaments collected over time. **THIS PAGE: 1.** This sea glass tree is one of the most popular holiday items at The Spotted Cod. **2.** A collection of vintage wicker flasks is on loan from Lee's friend Dee Askew during Christmas. **3.** An assortment of old seltzer bottles sport unique stoppers, including one made from a repurposed doorknob and sold in the shop. **4.** Lee fills matchboxes with tiny trinkets and trims them with paper and ribbon.

WHEN LEE REPETTO—a career-long retail stylist—first moved to Cape Cod, she vowed she'd avoid using nautical décor, considering it too predictable given the seaside location. "I wanted nothing to do with shells or nautical accents," laughs Lee, "but I soon changed my mind and grew to love it all and incorporated the style into our home." Situated in the historic town of Sandwich, Lee's home is a comfortable, welcoming place where she unwinds after long days spent working and greeting customers of her shop, The Spotted Cod (on 153 Main Street in Sandwich), a popular shopping destination for those seeking stylish home décor, authentic nautical collectibles like the Japanese fish floats that the shop is known for, and unique artwork and handcrafts by talented artisans from near to far. Visitors to the shop are quick to wax poetic about the "blue and green room," situated at the front of the store, where a sea-inspired color palette of watery hues wows all and is repeated in Lee's home. She works alongside her talented team, including her dearest friend and "right-hand" Dee Askew, to create stunning visual displays—especially at the holidays—and it is this knack for artful display that sets the stage in Lee's own home for a stylish holiday that is steeped in tradition.

SHADES OF AQUA Lee has a genuine love and affinity for all things aqua and her home and shop reflect it. **1.** The Spotted Cod is part of a stylish enclave of shops on Main Street in Sandwich. For information, call (508) 888-8263. **2.** Lee's holiday centers on family, friends, and her signature dishes, including snow pudding, a Fannie Farmer original recipe (Lee's great-grandmother was Fannie's assistant!). **3.** An old metal letter holder is filled with a collection of smalls, including a tiny book she holds dear—a gift from her grown daughter Allison, who eagerly heads home to the Cape each Christmas. **4.** Lee knew this old European clock would be hers the minute she spied it in a local antiques shop. Its original paint is a shade Lee dubs "dirty aqua," a color found throughout her home. **5.** Lee collects abandoned nests, like this one a friend found for her. **6.** A glass whale from The Spotted Cod rests atop a collection of old floats.

3

4

5

6

A SEA OF GLASS A collection of old bottles and Japanese fish floats line the windowsill in the dining area. Lee searches for unique bottle stoppers, both old and new, and receives regular shipments of the floats from Alaska to sell in her shop.

A QUIET SPOT A cedar wreath crowns an antique mirror made from an old window frame. Lee tucks away at the five-legged desk to catch up on paperwork for her shop. On the wall hangs a small Sailor's Valentine made by Sandy Moran.

BITS AND BOBS Christmas is a busy time on Cape Cod. Festive events, like tree-lighting ceremonies and holiday strolls, beckon locals and visitors alike and add to the magical holiday setting. When she can steal away from the bustle of her shop, Lee loves nothing more than taking brisk walks on the beach with her dog, Margo. Her holiday decorating is simple and uncluttered and always reflective of the coastal setting. A miniature Adirondack chair Lee brought home from her shop sports a tiny handmade wreath (above), made using local shells and beach glass.

HOLIDAY TREASURES

The holidays are a time to showcase cherished belongings. **1.** A tree ornament heralds the joy of the day. **2.** A tabletop deer sports a festive collar. **3.** A trio of swirled glass tree ornaments awaits hanging. **4.** Margo happily poses wearing a spiffy blue ribbon from the shop. Lee and her staff package up their customers' purchases in a craft box embellished with the signature trim. At Christmas, cheery red ribbon is used instead. **5.** Tiny wooden sail boats, a gift from the owners of the Nantucket shop Toy Boat, add a whimsical note. **6.** A miniature canoe holds a bottle brush tree dusted in faux snow. **7.** Tiny reindeer, passed down from her grandmother, are Lee's most treasured holiday ornaments. **8.** Lee sells these large wooden mermaids in her shop after giving them a verdigris finish.

Oh Happy Day!

"I like to keep my holiday décor simple, layering in treasured collectibles that my daughter Allison and I hold dear." — *Lee Repetto*

MESSAGE IN A BOTTLE

Lee and her team fill small vintage bottles (opposite) with sea glass and local sand to sell in the shop. They slip paper scrolls printed with holiday messages inside, and wrap them in twine to hang from tree boughs.

SWEET OFFERING

An afternoon of holiday shopping calls for some sugary sustenance. Lee bakes up brownies topped with icing and dragées and nestles them in cupcake liners for shop patrons to enjoy while they browse.

IN THE PINK

There's nothing expected about the mouth-watering colors and nostalgic decorations in blogger Koralee Teichroeb's holiday style—and that's why it's so much fun.

PRODUCED AND PHOTOGRAPHED BY
KORALEE TEICHROEB

Let your LiGHT SHINE

TRUE COLORS Blogger Koralee Teichroeb features what she calls "my pinks" and "my blues" in her fashion, food, and holiday décor, such as this mound of fuchsia carnations in a turquoise bowl (opposite), and the peppermint melties she makes and gives away (see recipe on page 234). She strings a tree with vintage pink ornaments and fabric swatches (this page), then melds it with a message chalked on an aqua-framed board.

AMONG KORALEE TEICHROEB'S FAVORITE THINGS are aprons, floral teacups, carnations, and baked goods. Sound familiar and comforting? Our Grandmothers would have loved the same things, but Koralee isn't trying to go back in time. Instead, she's dusting off these fond-but-forgotten staples and giving them places of honor in her bright, modern holiday decorating.

Readers of her blog BluebirdNotes.blogspot.com or her column in *Where Women Cook* magazine are already smitten with her food, photography, and inspiration sources, which she helpfully divides into singular categories: pinks, blues, and reds. "I'm very color oriented. I don't think I could live without pink," she says. "My home is all white but full of pops of turquoise and pink."

Those "pops" in Koralee's suburban Canadian home come in the form of a cerise desk chair or a cerulean bench. During the holidays, they appear in clusters of cheerful carnations or cake stands displaying ornaments. She doesn't stray from what makes her happy, she just gives it a holiday twist, like the peppermint melties she makes in her signature hues and gives away. The empty cookie tins and fabric swatches she finds at secondhand stores become packages for gifts and tree decorations. She stamps holiday greetings on plain note cards.

What some might dismiss as quaint relics of yesteryear, she makes part of her everyday style. With Koralee around, what's old is indeed new.

WITH STYLE TO SPARE Photography, food, decorating—"I am into everything," Koralee says. **1.** A schoolteacher and mother of three daughters, Koralee produces her blog, Bluebird Notes, from her home outside Vancouver, British Columbia **2.** Koralee's daughter Molly, 21, models her mom's garland. To make it, Koralee folded pieces of card stock, cut slits, then unfolded and wrapped them in cylinder shapes and hot-glued them to the light strand. **OPPOSITE:** Koralee's workspace is an old vanity table she bought secondhand and painted. She glued scraps of vintage wallpaper to the underside of the flip-up surface, and a band of fringe to the front.

HOME IMPROVEMENTS Anything can become holiday décor, Koralee says. **1.** She suspends pretty note cards from a lingerie drying rack that she snapped up because it is one of her favorite hues. **2.** Galvanized metal boxes become shadowboxes for holiday trinkets. **3.** To turn bookplate pockets into an advent calendar, Koralee first spray-paints the pockets with a figurine in front to create a shadow design, then she clips them to a string and adds treats. **4.** Koralee looks for striped socks, then tacks up three of her favorites as stockings for her daughters. "It's just a little tradition we have," she says. **5.** Tied up with ribbon and

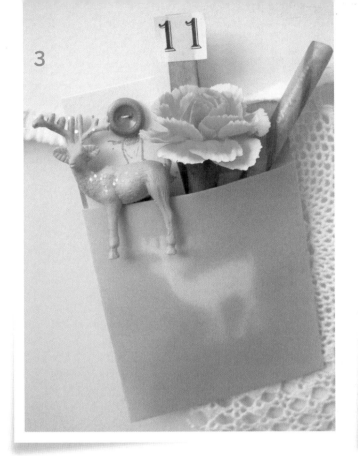

lace, timeworn tins become pretty gift packages. **6.** Year-round, she haunts the stationary section of secondhand stores. "I am in the Salvation Army every week, sometimes two times a week, finding the best vintage or recycled treasures," she says. She adds a holiday message using a date stamp. **7.** Dime-store figurines make unique gift decorations and cake toppers. **8.** Koralee's blogging pastime led to a book deal: The cookbook *Everything Goes with Ice Cream* will come out in spring 2013 from Quarry Books. In it, she features treats like this ice cream tower (see recipe on page 234), which she topped with melted white chocolate.

SIMPLY FUN Nothing is too serious in Koralee's house. **1.** She dresses up new bottlebrush trees by gluing on beads and glass trinkets. **2.** Pinecone ornaments, which prompted some of her passion for pink, are from her grandmother. **3.** Her collection of floral teacups doesn't match. **4.** A plate of treats tempts Santa. **OPPOSITE:** A fan of humble materials, Koralee tucks live carnation blooms into a faux wreath for an inexpensive live-flower touch. "Carnations are so versatile," she says. "You can do anything with them, and they tend to live and look lovely for a long time."

CELEBRATE

I have a giant ironstone punch bowl that I fill with
something special every year. Often, it's fizzy
cranberry punch or deliciously creamy spiced eggnog.
This year it will be the centerpiece of a dessert
buffet, where guests will ladle warm chocolate fondue from
its depths. We'll offer them a myriad of fruits,
cookies, and cakes to dunk and enrobe in it. I am looking
forward to staging this simplified gathering and
seeing the excitement of my friends and family as they
discover such a decadent treat. Whether you prepare an
entire meal or gather around a bowl filled with
melted chocolate, the act of celebrating and joining
together is what makes Christmas so magical.

SUNRISE BREAKFAST

Inside her elegant Brooklyn limestone home, Stefanie Schiada hosts family and friends for a hearty Christmas breakfast—perfect nourishment for a day filled to the brim with festivity.

FESTIVE FINERY AND FOOD

Rising early on Christmas morning is a natural reaction to such an exciting holiday. When hosting a breakfast gathering, plan your menu to include easy-to-prepare foods and keep the details elegant but simple. Stefanie layers her table with sheer silver fabric and lights candles and votives to reflect the sparkle of her favorite crystal and help illuminate a cold winter's morn. White dishes await waffles topped with fresh fruit and cream. OPPOSITE: Known for her attention to detail, Stefanie wrapped plain white napkin rings with birch paper and secured the ends with double-sided tape. You can copy the paper and napkin rings on page 255, or download them at HolidayWithMatthewMead.com.

CHRISTMAS MORNING STARTS EARLY for Luke and Stefanie Schiada—fondly known as Mr. and Mrs. Limestone by readers of her popular blog, BrooklynLimestone.com. Nestled on a quiet street, their century-old home—whose loving restoration is chronicled on the blog—greets guests eager to tuck into a breakfast of holiday comfort food. Stefanie confesses that the gathering combines two of her favorite things: designing and creating one-of-a-kind printed table favors, place cards, and gift tags—and entertaining. After long hours at her corporate day job, Stefanie feeds her creative spirit by flexing her entertaining chops and by spending some evenings devoted to her graphic design business (SonicStefDesign.com), known for what she calls "unexpected pieces for correspondence." She herself is a client: Says Stefanie, "In place of traditional Christmas cards, I design and create a little gift to send out to family and friends with our season's greetings. From custom-printed dishtowels to bookplates, I love the challenge of coming up with something new each year. It's how I always start my holiday engines." And the Schiadas' home is where friends love to gather. "Our renovation was a labor of love that resulted in a home that is perfect for us," says Stefanie, "and to be able to share Christmas morning here with those special to me is a holiday gift itself."

EAT, DRINK, AND BE MERRY THIS PAGE: Stefanie welcomes guests with a smile. A tray of glassware awaits filling: skewer fresh berries with hand-crafted drink stirrers to make guests' orange juice special. OPPOSITE: Stefanie was inspired to create a table favor after spotting rustic birch discs at the flower market. She designed and printed the greeting using her computer and transferred the image to the birch disc using t-shirt transfers and a hot iron. Find the stirrer and disc directions at HolidayWithMatthewMead.com.

SOPHISTICATED HOLIDAY STYLE

THIS PAGE: A sideboard painted in Martha Stewart's
Plumage offers display space for decorations,
drinks, and a collection of antique silver
candlesticks. Stefanie placed a mini Alberta Spruce,
its base wrapped in sheer silver fabric, in front of
a window for impact and trimmed it with mercury
ornaments. OPPOSITE: A glass vase holds branches,
silver ornaments, beads, and glittered foliage.
Paper star ornament directions can be found at
HolidayWithMatthewMead.com.

ALL THROUGH THE HOUSE **1.** A birch planter holds fresh greens, birch paper pinwheels, and star ornaments (directions at HolidayWithMatthewMead.com). **2.** The hall tree, original to the home, holds a birch cone filled with flowers and is the perfect spot for floral touches and gifts for guests. **3.** The kitchen island is a casual and easy place to arrange food buffet-style for easy replenishing. **4.** Tin boxes are filled with thoughtful food gifts from Stefanie's kitchen and the festive gift tags are her own design (copy them on page 255).

O TANNENBAUM After years of dragging a real tree home through the streets of their Brooklyn, New York, neighborhood, the Schiadas switched to a large, lush faux variety, but missed the natural scent. They solved their dilemma by showcasing a small, natural tree prominently on a vintage table. They decorated it with simple glass balls and paper ornaments (directions at HolidayWithMatthewMead.com), and its open location allows them to enjoy its festive fragrance without impeding traffic flow from room to room.

"I find Christmas morning so magical, and who doesn't just love breakfast foods?"
— *Stefanie Schiada*

QUICK AND TASTY 1. Make our tropical fruit salad or buy it ready-made from your grocer's deli. **2.** Pre-made Belgian waffles can be found in the bakery department of the grocery store. Heat gently in the oven and serve with fresh raspberries and whipped cream. **3.** Beignets, served with coffee and raspberry mimosas, are perfect breakfast finger foods. **4.** Make your own cinnamon buns or purchase a bake-and-serve variety and dress them up with orange cream cheese glaze (recipe below) and Christmas trees cut from orange peel. See page 234 for fruit salad and mimosa recipes.

ORANGE CREAM CHEESE GLAZE

You will need:

  2 cups cream cheese, at room temperature

  1 cup powdered sugar, sifted

  1/3 cup milk

  4 tablespoons fresh, grated orange zest;
  reserve two tablespoons for garnish.

1. In a medium bowl, place softened cream cheese and mix with hand mixer on medium speed until smooth.

2. Add in powdered sugar and milk alternately until thoroughly mixed.

3. Drop in orange zest and mix well.

4. Spread glaze over slightly warmed cinnamon buns and top with remaining orange zest.

ORANGE PEEL CHRISTMAS TREES

To make these fanciful orange Christmas trees, remove the peel from large sections of a thick-skinned orange. Using a 2-inch Christmas tree cookie cutter, cut out the festive shapes. Use a paring knife to clean up and sculpt the tree-shaped design. Refrigerate until ready to use as a garnish.

A SWEET LIFE

A colorful candy shop, the happy sounds of her children, and a generous serving of old-fashioned confection make for a sweet celebration of Stephanie Nielson's love of family, making fun new memories, and the holiday traditions she holds dear.

Nie Nie

HOLIDAY SWEETS

Smeeks candy shop, in Phoenix, Arizona, is a must-visit destination for candy lovers young and old. The shop sells everything from hard-to-find candy to toy novelties. Stephanie and her family stop in for a treat (or two!) whenever they are in town. Transform a store-bought layer cake (this page) with a simple but showy display of colorful candy nestled on top. Fill vintage butter pat dishes with a selection of white, blue, and red candy-coated chocolate-mint candies and have fun decorating your own customized holiday cake fit for a crowd.

CANDY BY THE POUND

The kitschy personality of Smeeks and its focus on fun appeals to Stephanie, and she knew it would make the perfect place to host a kids' holiday party. **1.** A dancing toy robot is a popular item at Smeeks. Here, Christian Nielson surprises the children with it. **2.** Rows and rows of candy, some favorites from eras gone by, are sought after by candy lovers of all ages. **3.** All sugared up, the Nielson children and their cousins deliver smiles and silliness. **4.** Create your own custom Smeeks holiday basket. Visit Smeeks.com for contact details or email smeeks.phoenix@gmail.com. **5.** Free gumballs ensure everyone leaves Smeeks with a sugary treat. **6.** Family friends Livvy and Avrey Jones share a hug. **7.** Paper straws are fun, old-fashioned novelties. **8.** Oliver Nielson offers to share a sugar cookie.

free treat! love, smeeks

COOKIES EVERYWHERE
Cookie artist Diane Knotek baked the snowflakes cookies (opposite) and these charming gnomes, which she intricately decorated with royal icing and a dusting of sugar crystals. Red and blue are the trademark colors used throughout the delightful shop, and the cheery palette can be found on everything from display cases to Smeeks's popular photo booth, where visitors happily pose for photos that are added to the shop's gallery wall. You'll find the snowflake cookie recipe starting on page 234 and the gnome pattern on page 253.

1

2

3

4

5

6

GINGERBREAD HOUSES

Claire and Jane present the beautifully detailed gingerbread house (opposite) created for the party by professional chef, Brendan McCaskey. The Nielson children create more modest versions with their parents each year, and it is just one of the traditions Stephanie loves to start the season with—knowing that holiday traditions make way for cherished family memories.

PARTY TIME

Nothing makes the holidays more magical than time spent just simply enjoying fun and silliness with friends and cousins.

1. Claire Nielson peeks out from behind a gingerbread house boasting cotton candy "chimney smoke."

2. Gingerbread houses can be decorated with just about any candy, including sticks of gum, candy wafers, strands of licorice, sour candy discs, striped peppermints, and more. The possibilities are as limitless as a child's imagination.

3. Little houses, crafted from graham wafers, are an easy alternative to baking gingerbread and are just as sturdy.

4. Jack DeWitt carefully decorates his gingerbread house as his cousins look on. Smeeks is available for parties for children "7 to 100 years old," in groups of up to ten people. Visit Smeeks.com for details.

5. Cal Nielson smiles with delight as he gets ready to enjoy a fizzy drink with his cousins.

6. The paper straws and soda pop at Smeeks conjure up memories of times gone by—when trips to the soda shop were few and far between, but always special. An adorable gnome cookie, in a coat of resplendent red, is almost too cute to eat. And while recreating a fancy cookie like this might be too daunting, the girls and Stephanie are no strangers to holiday baking. She, Claire, and Jane choose five new cookie recipes to try each December, and some end up as gifts for lucky recipients: "My little family has vowed to give only homemade gifts to each other; all other gifts come from Santa," shares Stephanie.

COOL, CALM, & COLLECTED

Hostess Sally McElroy creates an excuse for a relaxed, mid-season recess, invites some friends over, then puts her collections to use with an easy menu and fuss-free decorating.

SUBTLE SHADES
By sticking to a palette of silver, white, and pale green in her everyday decorating, Sally McElroy, a longtime friend of Matthew's, can easily step it up a notch for the holidays. She mixes new mercury glass candlesticks with a vintage silver stand holding orchid blooms (opposite). On the dining table (this page), champagne flutes are airy vases that don't block views across the table.

1 2

3 4

HOLIDAY ENTERTAINING SECRETS A practiced hostess, Sally prepares as much as she can in advance.
1. She toasts baguette slices in the oven before guests arrive, then asks someone to add the toppings. **2.** During the busy holidays, Sally relies on an easy-prep menu. And, rather than pull out holiday-specific tableware, she uses her everyday dishes and puts collections, such as these beloved cake stands, to use. **3.** A riot of Christmas color wouldn't do in Sally's spare kitchen. Instead, she got it party-ready with flowers and a mass of luscious apricots. **4.** Fresh cranberries give spinach salad a bite of seasonal flavor. **OPPOSITE:** A simple yet refined offering, this hearty chowder features chunks of lobster.

MENU

EDAMAME-PESTO BRUSCHETTA

CHEESY FLATBREAD

CRANBERRY-SPINACH SALAD

LOBSTER CHOWDER

DOUBLE CHOCOLATE COOKIES

PERFECT CHOCOLATE
GANACHE—TWO WAYS

Look for the recipes at
HOLIDAYWITHMATTHEWMEAD.COM
and starting on page 234.

USING COLLECTIBLES Like Matthew, Sally is an avowed fan of flea markets and estate sales, but can't just add more and more display cupboards in her home. So she puts her favorite finds—glass cake stands, silver serving dishes, and glass bottles—to work. For this cooking station (above), Sally cleans the bottles, adds new corks, and uses them to decant oils and vinegars. Vintage Shaker band boxes hold coarse salt and ground pepper. One remarkable find, a hand-blown bottle with a "Baccarat" stamp (opposite), cost her just $18 at a flea market. It moves around the house as a spot-on vase for garden blooms. At the holidays, Sally gives it extra panache by tying a cluster of dainty vintage ornaments around its neck.

LUNCHEON MADE EASY Far from stressful events, get-togethers like this seem to focus Sally on what's important. "Katie and I have been friends since our girls were two," she says. **1.** Mashed edamame and shaved Parmesan cheese are a savory bite atop crostini. **2.** Rather than serve courses, Sally puts nibbles along the center of the table. This vintage nut server wearing a wreath of thyme sprigs offers up olives. **3.** Friends exchange gifts and stories at Sally's holiday luncheon. **4.** A jug of water gets a special touch with slices of in-season citrus. **OPPOSITE:** To keep the meal preparation simple, Sally nests spinach salad into store-bought flatbreads.

SMALL GESTURES On a ledge-turned-gift table (opposite), Sally's cake stands sparkle in front of the windows. Stacking them creates a flexible display of silver mint julep cups and votive candleholders, which are filled with ornaments, hydrangeas, and holly leaves. "I love to entertain, and in a small house, it feels more intimate," she says. Asking a few girlfriends over to her turn-of-the-century cottage for a brief interlude in the hectic season is right up her alley. **1.** She wraps small gifts in pale green and white papers. To make the bow, she photocopied pages from an old journal (purchased at a flea market), rolled the copies into tubes, and hot-glued them in the center. A ball of tinsel finishes it off. **2.** At the close of the luncheon, there's nothing Sally's girlfriends want more than a trio of chocolate dessert choices, including crinkle cookies and ganache served as whipped mousse. **3.** She also spooned the ganache into mini-tart shells. All the recipes from Sally's get-together are available at HolidayWithMatthewMead.com, and starting on page 234.

FESTIVE FONDUE

A fondue party is a simple, fun way to indulge in a variety of sweet and savory foods without involving a lot of work—a perfect match for the bustle of the holidays. Assemble a tray of snickerdoodles, shortbread, coconut-filled candy, Pirouline cookies and more for dunking into a delicious pot of warm, melted chocolate.

APRÈS TREE

A cold day spent trudging through snow
in search of the perfect Christmas tree,
calls for a hearty pick-me-up of warm
chocolate, cheese, and all the trimmings.

1
2
3

WINTER WARM-UP

Stylist, blogger, and stationery artist Debra Norton (Etsy.com/Shop/VintagePaperParade) loves to throw casual get-togethers.
1. Christmas is very special to Debra, and she loves to entertain but still have time to enjoy her guests, too. A fondue party combines all of the elements Debra looks for when planning a party: good food, easy prep, and fun décor, like this pouf pillow made by stitching felt flowers to a ball pillow. **2.** Guests can warm their hands on generous mugs of apple cider (recipe page 234). Debra drew whimsical symbols on the mugs using a black porcelain pen, allowing for use year-round. But embellishing them with festive designs—like snowmen or Christmas trees—would look charming, too. **3.** Gingerbread cookies are a holiday classic and can be made in a variety of festive shapes. Debra got a head-start on planning her Christmas tree decorations by making these snowflake ornaments (opposite), made using white air-dry clay. She cut out the using her collection of cookie cutters, poked a hole in the top of each snowflake (to string later with red thread), and stamped a pattern in the ornaments using old rhinestone jewelry. Debra then left them to air-dry for two days before hanging. Visit Debra at VintagePaperParade. blogspot.com.

MARSHMALLOW WORLD

Wintry décor sets the stage: **1.** Debra made the wreath by wrapping yarn around a wooden form and Styrofoam™ balls, and then used hot glue to attach them. **2.** To make a paper stocking, trace a stocking shape onto two layers of newspaper and cut around the pattern. Stitch the two stocking pieces together and embellish using paper punch shapes and stickers. **3.** Fill wooden salt trays with sprinkles and nuts to top dipped sweets. **4.** Roast marshmallows over the flame of an unscented beeswax candle. **5.** Keep refills fresh by storing in a glass jar. **6.** Arrange the dessert fondue at its own station. **7.** Serve eggnog in glasses trimmed in fur cuffs. **8.** Dip the ends of candy apple sticks in red paint and use for dipping sweets. **OPPOSITE:** Top chocolate fondue with crumbled candy bars. See recipes beginning on page 234.

SAVORY BITES

Pairing cheese with chocolate appeals to everyone's decadent side, so be sure to have lots on hand! **1.** Guests will warm up fast when this gooey pot of melted cheddar fondue is placed in front of them (see recipe on page 234). Set out plenty of napkins, fondue forks, and edibles for dipping. **2.** To encourage mingling, arrange a stack of pewter bowls and plates so guests can help themselves to the cheesy goodness. **3.** Debra simplifies the party prep by purchasing quality meats from a deli, like this prosciutto she wrapped around thin breadsticks from a local bakery. Another mouth-watering dipping option is to roast a large elephant garlic bulb in the oven. To prepare, cut ¾ inch off the top of the garlic, drizzle it with olive oil, wrap in tinfoil, and bake in a 350 degree oven for 60 minutes. The mild garlic flavor lends itself well to specialty crackers and bread. Create a fondue pot (opposite) by arranging a cooling rack over a graniteware pan filled with unscented, non-toxic tea lights. A variety of baguettes, crackers, and steamed cauliflower and asparagus are ideal for dipping in the savory fondue. For the chocolate fondue, Debra uses packages of good-quality cookies and sweets that are holiday favorites, like chocolate-covered cherries and ginger cookies.

PENGUIN TREATS

There's nothing formal about this jolly children's party featuring tuxedo-clad cold-weather friends. You can recreate the bold decorations and yummy treats just by visiting a crafts store and our web site.

SET THE HAPPY SCENE
Bouquets of bright yellow balloons mark the treat buffet. Hang paper snowflakes and pinwheels from the ceiling, and array wrapped juice drinks, pudding cups, and dishes of candy around the cake. For the drink wraps, copy the pattern on page 254 or download it at HolidayWithMatthewMead. com. You can find paper snowflakes wherever party supplies are sold.

PAPER PINWHEELS

Pick up sheets of graphic yellow-and-white wrapping paper, and use them to fashion these pinwheels..

You will need:

    3 paper rectangles measuring 18x13 inches
    Double-stick tape

1. Starting on an 18-inch side, fold a rectangle in 1-inch, accordion-style pleats. Repeat for other two rectangles.

2. Bend each pleated rectangle in the middle to make three fan shapes. Place three fans together to form a circle.

3. Join the fans at the seams with tape.

TASTY TREATS Offer yellow candies, such as M&M®s or gumballs, and individual pudding cups. To make them, fill a clean, small crafts-store bucket with pudding up to a ½ inch from the top. Fill the remaining space with whipped cream, and smooth it using a water-moistened spatula. Cut a smaller circle out of parchment paper (we traced the bottom of the bucket) and lay it gently off-center on the whipped cream. Cover the remaining whipped cream with crushed chocolate-cookie crumbs. Remove the paper circle. Make the face using icing eyes, and eyebrows and a beak formed out of ready-made fondant from the crafts store.

MILK PUPPETS For these waddling sippers, use a funnel to fill empty soda or condiment containers with milk. You can reuse clean bottles or purchase new ones from a crafts store or restaurant supply store. Download the wings template from HolidayWithMatthewMead.com, or turn to page 254, and cut them from black construction paper; stick them on with double-sided tape. Top each bottle with a head made from a chocolate donut hole. Icing eyes and small fondant beaks—materials available at the crafts store—complete the penguin face. Finally, wrap a scarf of mini-ball fringe.

1. PARTY PREP

Have fun embellishing your rooms with decorations and games that fit the theme. These paper balloons are Japanese children's toys we found online; they can be used again and again. At party supply stores, you'll also find penguin piñatas and mylar balloons. While you're there, stock up on cups, plates and napkins that fit the color theme. Choosing colorful polka-dot dinnerware—rather than character-themed paper goods—allows you to re-use them for another event or party.

2. LET THEM EAT CAKE

The centerpiece of your treats table is this dashing penguin cake.

You will need:

Your favorite cake mix
1 container chocolate frosting
Black icing color, such as Wilton®
8-inch round cake stencil
8 ounces desiccated coconut
Ready-made fondant in black, yellow, and tan

1. Bake two 9-inch cakes according to package directions. Let cool.

2. Use concentrated icing color to tint chocolate frosting black. Frost cake layers. To get a smooth, shiny surface, dip your metal spatula in warm water as you smooth the frosting.

3. Place a round cake stencil over the cake off-center, and fill the area with desiccated coconut, which is dried, finely flaked coconut from the baking aisle of the grocery store.

4. Add icing eyes and fondant decorations. To make the polka dots for the bow tie, roll out ready-made yellow fondant and punch circles using pastry bag tips.

3. HOME PLATE

No need to invest in specialty dinnerware for the party. Just personalize a plain plate by layering our cute penguin paper face on top of the plate and under a smaller glass salad plate. Copy the inserts on page 254 or download them from HolidayWithMatthewMead.com.

4. FROSTY BIRDS

Make your own push pops by purchasing the plastic containers that you can fill with any blend of frozen confection.

You will need:

Push pop containers (from an online specialty food store)
Pudding in flavors banana, chocolate, and white chocolate
Black food color
Black paper
Penguin stickers

1. Tint chocolate pudding black using food coloring.

2. Layer banana, black-tinted chocolate, and white chocolate pudding in containers.

3. Wrap bands of black paper around the containers and affix with double-sided tape.

4. Freeze overnight. Just before the party, add penguin stickers.

ENTERTAINMENT PICKS

GAMES Play "Pin the Beak on the Penguin" using a wildlife poster from a museum or zoo shop, or make your own using black markers, white poster board, and orange construction paper beaks. Other timeless favorites, such as Musical Chairs, can be updated with a penguin theme. Ask the kids to waddle around the circle until they find seats. Or, play the variation: Duck, Duck, Penguin!

MOVIES In the background of the festivities, show *March of the Penguins* (rated G, 2005), *Happy Feet* (rated PG, 2006), or *Mr. Popper's Penguins* (rated PG, 2011).

MUSIC Soundtracks for the movies mentioned above make great background tunes, and songs can be stopped and started for a rousing rendition of Musical Chairs. Look also for the soundtrack for the recent movie, *Happy Feet Two* in 3D.

1

2

3

4

THE COMPLETE PACKAGE Guests won't be able to resist these welcoming invitations (ABOVE, LEFT). Download them from HolidayWithMatthewMead.com and print them on card stock. Punch two holes for threading the ball-fringe scarf, and a hole at the top for a garnish of twine.

CUTE SIPPERS For these juice drink wraps (ABOVE, RIGHT), we've done the work for you. Visit our web site, download the pre-sized designs, and you can even add the names from your guest list using Adobe®PhotoShop®. Not sure who's coming yet? Copy the wraps from page 254, then rub on letter decals from the crafts store at the last minute.

TAKE-AWAY GIFTS

As the party winds down, stack up a variety of empty gift boxes and invite guests to fill them with their choice of take-home treats, such as desserts, candy, balloons, and snowflake decorations.

recipes

STORYBOOK CHRISTMAS

ROYAL ICING

You will need:

- 1 pound (1 box) powdered sugar, sifted (4½ cups)
- 3 tablespoons meringue powder
- ½ teaspoon cream of tartar
- ½ cup warm water
- 1 teaspoon vanilla extract

1. In a medium mixing bowl, whisk together the powdered sugar, meringue powder, and cream of tartar.

2. Add the water and vanilla extract; beat with an electric mixer on low speed until combined. Beat on high speed for 7 to 10 minutes, or until the mixture is very stiff.

3. Refrigerate in an airtight container for 2 to 3 days.

Makes 3 cups

BOILED ICING SNOWMEN

You will need:

- 2 cups white sugar
- 1 cup water
- 1 pinch salt
- 1 teaspoon distilled white vinegar
- 2 egg whites
- ¾ teaspoon vanilla extract

1. In a small saucepan, combine sugar, water, salt, and vinegar. Cook over medium heat, stirring constantly, just until mixture is clear. Then continue cooking without stirring until the syrup reaches 240° on a candy thermometer, or until it spins a long thread when dropped from the tip of a spoon.

2. In a medium mixing bowl, beat egg whites using an electric mixer on high speed until soft peaks form. Add syrup in a very thin stream, beating constantly. After all the syrup is added, continue beating until icing will hold its shape. Mix in vanilla.

3. Fill a pastry bag fitted with a round tip with icing. Pipe snowballs in several sizes onto a parchment-paper-lined baking sheet, about 1 inch apart.

4. Let snowballs air dry in a cool dry place for several days until thoroughly dried. Assemble snowmen, using piping gel from the cake-decorating aisle of the crafts store to hold snowballs together, and to attach decorations, such as non-pareils, fruit rubber, and gumdrops.

5. To make the Santas, follow recipe for boiled icing, but use different piping tips on the pastry bag to form a flatter shape. Tint batches of the icing using gel food coloring from the crafts store to get the red and flesh colors.

ANGELS

GINGERBREAD ANGELS

You will need:

- ½ cup butter
- ½ cup granulated sugar
- ½ cup molasses
- 1 egg yolk
- 2 cups all-purpose flour, sifted
- ½ teaspoon salt
- ½ teaspoon baking powder
- ½ teaspoon baking soda
- ½ teaspoon ground cinnamon
- 1 teaspoon ground cloves
- 1 teaspoon ginger
- ½ teaspoon ground nutmeg

Preheat oven to 350°

1. In a large mixing bowl, cream together the butter and sugar using an electric mixer on high speed until smooth. Stir in molasses and egg yolk.

2. In a medium-size mixing bowl, combine flour, salt, baking powder, baking soda, cinnamon, cloves, ginger, and nutmeg. Add flour mixture to the molasses mixture and blend until smooth. Cover, and chill for at least one hour.

3. On a lightly floured surface, roll the dough out to ¼-inch thickness. Cut into desired shapes with cookie cutters. Place cookies 2 inches apart on ungreased cookie sheets. Use a skewer to create ¼-inch holes in each shoulder of the cookie.

4. Bake for 8 to 10 minutes until firm. Let cookies cool on pans for 2 minutes, then remove them to wire racks to cool completely. Dot the cookies with royal icing buttons (see recipe on page 234). When dry, tie on paper wings using kitchen twine.

Makes 2½ dozen cookies

HEAVENLY SPICE CAKE

You will need:
CAKE

- 3 cups all-purpose flour
- 3 ½ teaspoons baking powder
- 2 teaspoons pumpkin pie spice
- 1 teaspoon ground ginger
- 1 teaspoon baking soda
- ¾ teaspoon ground nutmeg
- ½ teaspoon salt
- 1 ½ cups granulated sugar
- 1 ½ sticks butter, softened
- 3 large eggs

1 ½ cups canned puréed pumpkin

½ cup evaporated milk

¼ cup water

1 ½ teaspoons vanilla extract

ICING

11 ounces cream cheese (an 8-ounce package plus a 3-ounce package), softened

⅓ cup butter, softened

3 ½ cups powdered sugar, sifted

3 tablespoons ground cinnamon

Preheat oven to 325°

1. Grease and flour two 8-inch square cake pans.

2. In a small bowl, combine flour, baking powder, pumpkin pie spice, ginger, baking soda, nutmeg, and salt and set aside.

3. In a large bowl, beat sugar and butter using an electric mixer on high speed until creamy. Add eggs; beat for 2 minutes. Beat in pumpkin, evaporated milk, water, and vanilla extract. Gradually beat in flour mixture. Spread evenly into prepared cake pans.

4. Bake for 35 to 40 minutes, or until wooden pick inserted in center comes out clean. Cool in pans on wire racks for 15 minutes; remove cakes from pans and place on wire racks to cool completely.

5. For the icing, beat cream cheese, butter, and powdered sugar in large mixing using an electric mixer on high speed bowl until fluffy.

6. To decorate frosted cake, place stencil in the center, sprinkle ground cinnamon over top of stencil and cake. Remove stencil. (Use a stencil of your choosing, or download this one from HolidayWithMatthewMead.com.)

CANDY, PAPER, SCISSORS

CANDY-STUDDED CHOCOLATE COOKIES

You will need:

1 cup semi-sweet chocolate chips

3 large egg whites, at room temperature

2 ½ cups confectioner's sugar, divided

½ cup unsweetened cocoa powder

1 tablespoon cornstarch

¼ teaspoon salt

2 cups small red candies or candy-coated chocolates

Preheat oven to 400°

1. Grease two 9x13-inch baking sheets with vegetable spray.

2. In a glass bowl, melt 1 cup of chocolate chips in the microwave, stirring every 30 seconds for about 2 minutes, or until melted. Let cool slightly.

3. Using a stand mixer set on high speed, beat egg whites until soft peaks form, then slowly add 1 cup sugar. Continue beating until mixture resembles soft marshmallow cream.

4. In a separate medium bowl, whisk together cocoa, cornstarch, salt, and 1 cup of powdered sugar.

5. Turning the mixer to low speed, add the dry ingredients into the egg mixture. Add in the cooled chocolate. At this point, the dough will become very stiff.

6. Place ½ cup powdered sugar in a small bowl. Roll 1 rounded tablespoon of dough into a ball; roll in sugar, coating thickly. Place on greased baking sheet.

7. Repeat with remaining dough, spacing balls 2-inches apart. Bake for about 10 minutes, or until the cookies are puffed and their tops crack. Remove from oven and press candy into tops of cookies. Let cool on baking sheets for 10 minutes. Transfer to rack; continue to let cool.

Makes about 24 cookies

HOLIDAY COOKIES

GINGER COOKIES WITH ROYAL ICING
Recipe adapted from Around My French Table *by Dorie Greenspan (Houghton Mifflin Harcourt; 2010)*

You will need:

7 tablespoons salted butter

½ cup granulated sugar

½ cup brown sugar

1 large egg

1 ⅔ cup flour

¼ teaspoon salt

¼ teaspoon baking soda

2 teaspoons cinnamon

½ teaspoon ground ginger

¼ teaspoon ground cloves

Preheat oven to 350°

1. In a stand mixer, cream the butter with the sugars until fluffy.

2. Add the egg and beat, then add the flour, salt, baking soda, and spices in three batches, beating between each addition until just combined.

3. Divide the dough into two, form each piece of dough into a flat disk, and chill until firm.

4. Roll out each disk of dough to about ¼-inch thickness, and use a cookie cutter to cut out. Transfer the cut out cookies to a cookie sheet lined with a silicone mat, and bake for 10 minutes. Cool on a wire rack before decorating.

For the royal icing, you will need:

- 4 tablespoons meringue powder
- ½ cup water
- 1 pound powdered sugar
- 1 teaspoon light corn syrup water

1. Combine the meringue powder and water in the bowl of a stand mixer. Using the paddle attachment, beat until foamy. Switch to low speed and sift in the powdered sugar, and beat to combine. Add the corn syrup, and beat for about 5 minutes until stiff peaks form.

2. Put the stiff icing into an icing bag fitted with a plain round #3 tip. (You can also put icing into a sealable plastic bag, and snip off a small corner.) Pipe the designs around each cookie.

JAM THUMBPRINTS
Recipe by Mary O'Brien

You will need:

- ⅔ cup unsalted butter, room temperature
- ⅓ cup granulated sugar
- 2 egg yolks
- 1 teaspoon vanilla
- ½ teaspoon salt
- 1½ cups all-purpose flour
- 2 egg whites, slightly beaten
- ¾ cup walnuts, finely chopped
- ¾ cup seedless jam, such as raspberry, strawberry, or apricot

Preheat oven to 350°

1. In a large mixing bowl, cream together butter and sugar, using an electric mixer on high speed, till light and fluffy. Add egg yolks, vanilla, and salt. Beat well, then switch to low speed and gradually add flour until dough forms.

2. Shape into 1-inch balls, dip them in the egg whites, and then roll balls in the walnuts, covering the entire surface of

each cookie. Place 1 inch apart on greased cookie sheet. Press center of each cookie with thumb to make imprint.

3. Bake for 15 to 17 minutes. Let cookies cool 2 minutes on baking sheet, then transfer to wire rack. While still warm, fill imprints with jam. Let cool completely.

Makes 3 dozen cookies

ALMOND FINANCIERS WITH BLACKBERRY JAM
Recipe adapted from DorieGreenspan.com

You will need:

- 12 tablespoons salted butter
- 1 cup sugar
- 1 cup almond flour
- 6 egg whites
- ⅔ cup flour
- 2 tablespoons blackberry jam

Preheat oven to 400 degrees

1. In a small saucepan, heat the butter until it gives off a nutty aroma and is a deep golden brown color. Let cool.

2. Combine the sugar, almond flour, and egg whites in a saucepan. Heat over low heat, stirring constantly, until the mixture is pale, runny and hot. Blend in the flour and the browned butter, which will not want to incorporate but will, after much stirring. Chill the batter until cold. It will be quite firm.

3. Grease the financier molds or mini-muffin tins with a butter-flour spray, or butter and flour each mold. Fill each mold just to the top with batter and scrape out any excess. Spoon dabs of blackberry jam into the center of each financier.

4. Bake for 13 minutes, or until the tops are crisp and browned. Remove from the molds and cool.

SALTY PEANUT SQUARES
Recipe by Grant Matthews

You will need:
CRUST:

- 3 cups plus 2 tablespoons all-purpose flour
- 1 cup packed brown sugar
- 1 teaspoon kosher salt
- 2 sticks plus 6 tablespoons unsalted butter, chilled and cut into pieces

FILLING:

- 2 sticks unsalted butter
- ¼ cup granulated sugar
- 1½ cups plus 2 tablespoons packed brown sugar
- ½ cup honey
- ¼ cup plus 1 tablespoon whipping cream
- ¼ teaspoon kosher salt
- 1 teaspoon vanilla
- 3½ cups roasted salted peanuts

Preheat oven to 350°

1. Form a foil liner for a 15x10-inch baking pan with 1-inch sides by inverting the pan and molding a sheet of aluminum foil over the bottom and sides. Flip the pan back over, grease it, and fit the foil liner into the pan. Grease the foil. Set aside.

2. For the crust, place the flour, brown sugar, and salt in a food processor with a steel blade, and pulse to blend. Add the butter and pulse a few more times until the dough just starts to come together—do not let the dough form a ball. Evenly press the dough into the bottom and up the sides of the prepared pan. Place the pan in the refrigerator and chill the dough until firm; about 30 minutes. (The crust can be prepared 2 days ahead of time.)

3. Bake the crust for 25 to 30 minutes, until lightly browned, rotating the pan halfway through baking time. Check the crust periodically, and if it's puffing up, press it down gently with a fork.

4. For the filling, combine the butter, both sugars, and honey in a large saucepan and cook over medium heat, whisking continually, until it boils. Boil for 3 minutes, whisking continually. Remove from heat and add the cream, salt, vanilla, and peanuts. Pour the filling over the baked crust, spreading evenly.

5. Bake 25 to 30 minutes until filling is evenly bubbling and golden—not dark—brown. The filling will appear fairly set when pan is shaken. Remove from oven; allow to cool completely in the pan.

6. To cut the bars, grasp the foil liner; pull up to loosen foil from pan. Cover bars with a baking sheet and turn over. Peel foil liner off crust. Cover the bars with a second baking sheet and turn onto a cutting surface. Cut them into 1¼ -inch squares. These can be stored in a freezer for up to 3 months.

Makes about 7 dozen squares

DULCE DE LECHE CRISPY-RICE-CEREAL TREATS
Recipe by Kate Wheeler at Savour-Fare.com

You will need:
- 1 10-ounce package marshmallows
- 3 tablespoons salted butter
- 6 cups crispy rice cereal
- ½ cup prepared dulce de leche sauce, such as Nestlé®

1. Grease a 9X13-inch rectangular pan with butter.

2. In a large pot, combine the butter and marshmallows, and cook over low heat until the marshmallows are melted and the butter is incorporated. Immediately mix in the rice cereal.

3. Spread the cereal mixture into the prepared pan. Dollop large spoonfuls of dulce de leche sauce irregularly over the cereal mixture, then spread to cover.

4. Chill in the refrigerator, and cut with a sharp knife. Decorate as desired.

TRIPLE CHOCOLATE ALMOND BISCOTTI
Recipe by Debbie Smith

You will need:
BISCOTTI:
- 2 cups all-purpose flour
- 1 ½ teaspoons baking powder
- ½ teaspoon salt
- 1 stick butter
- 1 ¼ cups granulated sugar
- ½ cup unsweetened cocoa powder
- 2 eggs
- 2 teaspoons vanilla
- ¾ cup slivered almonds, chopped
- 1 cup mini-chocolate chips

DRIZZLE:
- 8 ounces white almond bark

Preheat oven to 350°

1. Sift together flour, baking powder, and salt in a small bowl; set aside. Beat butter, sugar, and cocoa powder in a large mixing bowl, using an electric mixer on high speed, until light and fluffy. Add eggs, vanilla, and flour mixture. Mix will, and fold in the chocolate chips and almonds.

2. Shape the dough into two logs and place on parchment-paper-lined baking sheets. Bake for 35 to 40 minutes.

3. Reduce heat in oven to 250°. Cut logs into ½-inch-thick slices and bake again until desired crispness, about 20 to 25 minutes. Place on wire racks to cool.

4. Melt almond bark according to package directions. Dip in a spoon and drizzle melted white chocolate over the cool biscotti.

Makes 8 large biscotti

CHOCOLATE-DIPPED PEANUT BUTTER COOKIES
Recipe by Lizzy Reschke

You will need:
COOKIES:
- 1¼ cups all-purpose flour
- ½ teaspoon baking soda
- ½ teaspoon baking powder
- ¼ teaspoon salt
- 1 stick butter
- ½ cup peanut butter
- ½ cup granulated sugar, plus ¼ cup extra for rolling
- ½ cup firmly packed brown sugar
- ½ teaspoon vanilla
- 1 egg

COATING:
- 2 cups semi-sweet chocolate chips
- 1 tablespoon shortening

Preheat oven to 375°

1. In a small bowl, sift together flour, baking soda, baking powder, and salt; set aside.

2. In a large mixing bowl, beat together butter, peanut butter, ½ cup granulated sugar, and brown sugar using an electric mixer on high speed until smooth. Add vanilla, egg, and then the flour mixture until well combined.

3. Shape the dough into 1-inch balls and roll them in extra sugar. Flatten the dough balls with a fork in a criss-cross design.

4. Bake 8 to 9 minutes. Let cookies cool for 1 minute on baking sheets, then transfer to cooling racks to cool completely.

5. For the coating, melt chocolate chips and shortening in a small heavy saucepan on medium head, stirring frequently until melted and smooth. Remove from heat. Dip half the cookie into the melted chocolate. Place on wax paper until chocolate has set.

Makes 2½ dozen cookies

CHOCOLATE WALNUT WHEELS
Recipe by Amelia Huntington

You will need:

- ⅓ cup unsalted butter, room temperature
- 1 cup granulated sugar
- 1 egg
- 2 squares unsweetened chocolate, melted
- ¼ teaspoon vanilla
- ⅔ cup cake flour, sifted
- ¼ teaspoon salt
- 1 cup walnuts, minced walnut halves

Preheat oven to 350°

1. In a large mixing bowl, cream together butter and sugar, using an electric mixer on high speed. Gradually add egg, melted chocolate, and vanilla. Add flour, salt and nuts, and beat well.

2. Use a teaspoon to drop dough an inch apart onto a parchment-paper-lined baking sheet. Press a walnut half into the top of each cookie.

3. Bake for 10 minutes. Remove cookies from sheet and cool on a wire rack.

Makes 2 dozen cookies

CHOCOLATE THUMBPRINTS
Recipe by Tina Wheeler

You will need:
COOKIES:

- 2 cups all-purpose flour
- 1 cup plus 1 tablespoon unsweetened Dutch-process cocoa powder
- 2 teaspoons coarse salt
- 2 sticks unsalted butter, softened
- 1 ⅓ cups granulated sugar, plus more for rolling
- 2 large egg yolks
- 2 tablespoons heavy cream
- 2 teaspoons vanilla

GANACHE FILLING:

- ⅓ cup honey
- ⅓ cup heavy cream

- Half a vanilla bean, split and scraped, pod reserved
- 4 ounces bittersweet chocolate, finely chopped
- 1 ounce (2 tablespoons) unsalted butter, cut into pieces and softened

Preheat oven to 350°

1. For the cookies, sift flour, cocoa powder, and salt together in a small bowl. In a separate large mixing bowl, cream butter and sugar with an electric mixer on high speed until pale and fluffy. Reduce speed to medium, and add yolks, cream, and vanilla. Scrape sides of bowl. Beat in flour mixture until just combined.

2. Roll dough into 2-inch balls, and roll each in sugar. Place an inch apart on parchment-lined baking sheets. With the handle of a wooden spoon, press gently in the center of each to create an indentation.

3. Bake about 10 minutes, rotating sheets halfway through, until cookies are set. If indentations lose definition, press centers again. Let cool for 1 minute on baking sheets. Transfer cookies to wire racks, and let cool completely.

4. For ganache filling: Combine honey, cream, and the vanilla seeds and pod in a medium saucepan over medium heat. Bring to a simmer and cook, stirring, until honey dissolves. Remove from heat, cover, and let stand for 20 minutes. Place chocolate in a food processor. Return cream mixture to a simmer, and then strain through a fine sieve. Discard solids. Pour cream mixture over chocolate, and let stand for 1 minute. Process until smooth. Add butter, and continue to process, scraping down sides occasionally, until butter is incorporated.

6. Spoon warm ganache into center of each cookie. Let stand until firm, about 15 minutes. Store in an airtight container for up to 3 days.

Makes about 7½ dozen cookies

GRANDMA'S BOURBON BALLS
Recipe by Kate Wheeler
at Savour-Fare.com

You will need:

- 10 ounces graham crackers, crushed into fine crumbs
- 1 cup walnut halves, ground finely in a food processor
- ½ cup confectioner's sugar
- 6 ounces semi-sweet chocolate chips
- ½ cup bourbon
- 3 tablespoons golden syrup or light corn syrup
- Extra granulated sugar or decorative sanding sugar

1. Combine cookie crumbs, ground walnuts and confectioner's sugar in a large mixing bowl.

2. In a glass bowl, heat the chocolate chips for 30 seconds, then in 10 second intervals, stirring between each interval, until the chips are mostly melted. They'll melt as you stir. Add in bourbon and corn syrup and stir to combine (the chocolate will seize a bit, and the bourbon won't incorporate well. Just do the best you can).

3. Add the chocolate mixture to the crumbs mixture, and stir until thoroughly combined. Chill at least 30 minutes.

4. Pour granulated sugar or decorative sanding sugar into a dish. Form the chocolate mixture into small balls the size of grapes, and roll each ball in the sugar. Store for up to a month in a lidded container.

AUSTRIAN CHOCOLATE BALLS
Recipe by Janet Dubuc

You will need:
COOKIES:

- 2 squares unsweetened chocolate
- ⅓ cup butter
- 1 cup granulated sugar
- 1 egg, plus 1 yolk
- ½ teaspoon vanilla
- 1 ⅓ cup all-purpose flour
- ½ cup finely nuts, finely chopped

GLAZE:

1 square unsweetened chocolate

1 tablespoon butter

¼ teaspoon vanilla

1 cup powdered sugar

2 to 3 tablespoons milk

Preheat oven to 350°

1. In a small saucepan over medium heat, melt together 2 squares of chocolate and ⅓ cup of butter. When smooth, pour into a large mixing bowl. Add granulated sugar, egg and yolk, and ½ teaspoon vanilla, and stir with a wooden spoon until well combined. Add flour and nuts, and gradually stir until just combined.

2. Shape dough into 1-inch balls and place on ungreased baking sheet about 1 inch apart.

3. Bake for 8 to 12 minutes, until balls are firm to the touch. Move cookie balls to wire rack immediate to cool completely.

4. For the glaze, melt 1 square of chocolate and 1 tablespoon of butter in small saucepan over medium heat until smooth. Remove from heat and stir in remaining glaze ingredients. Dip tops of cookies into glaze to cover. Allow to set completely.

Makes 4 dozen cookies

CRANBERRY FLORENTINES
Recipe by Kate Wheeler
at Savour-Fare.com

You will need:

½ cup heavy cream

½ cup granulated sugar

4 tablespoons butter, divided

1 cup sliced almonds

½ cup dried cranberries

2 tablespoons chopped candied orange peel (optional)

⅓ cup flour

¼ cup chocolate chips

Preheat oven to 350 degrees

1. In a saucepan, combine the cream, sugar, and 3 tablespoons butter and bring to a boil. Add the almonds, cranberries, orange peel, and flour, and stir to combine.

2. Drop the cookies by the teaspoon at least 2 inches apart on a baking sheet lined with a silicone mat. These spread considerably during baking, so place them at least 3 inches apart.

3. Bake for 8-10 minutes, or until the edges of the cookies are brown and crisp. Let cool on the cookie sheets for 5 minutes, then carefully remove to a wire rack.

4. Melt the chocolate chips with the remaining 1 tablespoon butter in a microwave-safe bowl, by heating for 30 seconds, then at 10 second intervals, stirring between each interval, until the mixture is smooth. Drizzle the chocolate over the cooled cookies.

FIVE-SPICE SNAILS
Recipe by Kate Wheeler
at Savour-Fare.com

You will need:

1 sheet frozen puff pastry

½ cup granulated sugar

2 teaspoons Chinese 5-spice powder

Preheat oven to 350 degrees

1. Let the puff pastry thaw completely in the refrigerator. Sprinkle sugar on your work surface and sprinkle some spice powder over it. Lay the chilled pastry on the work surface, sprinkle with spice and sugar, fold lengthwise into thirds. Sprinkle more sugar and spice on the pastry and roll out into a thin rectangle, about 13X15 inches, pressing the spice and sugar into the dough. Sprinkle more sugar and spice over the dough, then roll up into a spiral on the long side. Wrap the spiral in plastic wrap and chill.

2. Slice the spiral log into ½-inch slices and arrange on a cookie sheet lined with parchment paper. Bake 13-15 minutes, or until crisp and the pastry is baked through.

MAPLE NUT COOKIES
Recipe by Maggie Grussing

You will need:
COOKIES:

2 cups all-purpose flour

½ teaspoon baking soda

1 teaspoon salt

¼ teaspoon ground nutmeg

1 teaspoon ground cinnamon

1 stick butter, softened

1 cup granulated sugar

2 ounces reduced-fat cream cheese

¼ cup unsweetened applesauce

1 egg

1 tablespoon skim milk

½ teaspoon vanilla extract

½ teaspoon maple extract

¾ cup chopped walnuts

½ cup cinnamon chips

½ semisweet chocolate chips

GLAZE:

2 tablespoons skim milk

2 teaspoons real maple syrup

2 cups powdered sugar, or enough to get glaze to stiffen

Preheat oven to 375°

1. Sift together flour, baking soda, salt, nutmeg, and cinnamon in a small bowl and set aside.

2. In a large mixing bowl, cream together butter and sugar; add softened cream cheese and applesauce. Mix on medium speed until just blended, then add the egg and mix again. Next add milk, vanilla extract, and maple extract; mix until just combined. Switch to low speed and slowly add flour mixture. Finally, stir in the walnuts, cinnamon chips, and chocolate chips with a wooden spoon.

3. Roll 1-inch balls of dough and place 1 to 2 inches apart on a parchment-paper-lined baking sheet. Bake 15 to 18 minutes. Let cookies cool on the baking sheet for 3 minutes, then transfer to a wire rack to finish cooling.

4. For glaze, stir together milk and syrup, then add powdered sugar, stirring with a whisk, until it reaches consistency of syrup. Dip in a spoon and drizzle over cooled cookies.

Makes 3 dozen cookies

CITRUS HAZELNUT FINGERS
Recipe by Olivia Newbery

You will need:

> 1½ cups hazelnuts
>
> 1 cup unsalted butter, softened
>
> ½ cup superfine granulated sugar
>
> 2 teaspoons vanilla
>
> 2 teaspoons finely shredded orange peel
>
> 2 cups all-purpose flour
>
> 6 ounces semisweet chocolate, chopped
>
> 1 teaspoon shortening
>
> 3 ounces milk chocolate, chopped
>
> ½ teaspoon shortening

Preheat oven to 350°

1. Place hazelnuts in a shallow baking pan and bake for 13 to 14 minutes or until golden brown and fragrant. While still warm, rub briskly in a folded-over clean kitchen towel to remove most of the skins from the nuts. Place nuts in a food processor fitted with a steel blade. Cover and process until nuts are finely ground; set aside.

2. Place butter in a large mixing bowl and beat with an electric mixer on high speed for 30 seconds. Add sugar, vanilla, and orange peel and beat until mixture is light and fluffy. Beat in ground hazelnuts until combined. Beat in as much of the flour as you can with the mixer. Stir in any remaining flour.

3. Roll tablespoon-size portions of dough into 2-inch finger shapes. Place fingers 2 inches apart on an ungreased cookie sheet

4. Bake for 12 to 14 minutes, or until edges begin to brown. Cool 1 minute on cookie sheet. Transfer fingers to wire racks to cool completely.

5. In a small heavy saucepan melt semisweet chocolate and 1 teaspoon shortening over low heat. Dip half of each cooled cookie into chocolate mixture to coat, allowing excess to drip off. Place cookies on waxed paper to cool until chocolate is set.

6. In a small heavy saucepan melt milk chocolate and ½ teaspoon shortening over low heat. With a spoon or whisk, drizzle chocolate over cookies. Store in an airtight container for up to 3 days.

Makes 4 dozen cookies

CRANBERRY & DARK CHOCOLATE-CHIP COOKIES
Recipe by Sarah Bradford

You will need:

> 1 cup coconut oil at warm room temperature
>
> ½ cup organic whole cane sugar
>
> 2 eggs
>
> ½ teaspoon salt
>
> ½ teaspoon baking powder
>
> ½ cup all-purpose gluten-free baking flour
>
> ½ teaspoon allspice
>
> ½ cup raw creamy unsalted almond butter
>
> ½ cup dark chocolate chips
>
> ½ cup dried cranberries
>
> ½ cup shredded coconut
>
> ¾ cup old-fashioned oats, plus more as needed until the dough is not too sticky to handle

Preheat oven to 400°

1. In a large mixing bowl, combine coconut oil and sugar and stir with a wooden spoon until smooth. Add in eggs, salt, baking powder, flour, and allspice, and stir until combined. Add almond butter and stir until mixture is shiny and sticky. Then stir in remaining ingredients, using your hands to form the dough if necessary.

2. Form 1-inch balls of dough and place on a parchment-paper-lined baking sheet about 2 inches apart. Press two fingers into the ball to flatten into a round cookie.

3. Bake for about 8 to 10 minutes. Transfer the cookies to a rack to cool completely.

LEMON DROP COOKIES
Recipe by Angie Perrazzino

You will need:
COOKIES:

> 3½ cups all-purpose flour, plus extra if needed
>
> 2 teaspoons baking powder
>
> 1 teaspoon baking soda
>
> 1/8 teaspoon salt
>
> 1 cup unsalted butter, melted and cooled
>
> 2 cups granulated sugar
>
> 2 eggs
>
> 1 teaspoon pure lemon oil
>
> Zest of 1 lemon
>
> 16 ounces whole-milk ricotta, drained

GLAZE:

> 2 large egg whites
>
> 2 cups powdered sugar, sifted
>
> 1 to 1½ tablespoons fresh-squeezed lemon juice
>
> ¼ teaspoon pure lemon oil

Preheat oven to 375°

1. In a large bowl, sift together flour, baking powder, baking soda, and salt; set aside. 2. In a large mixing bowl, beat butter and sugar using an electric mixer on high-speed until smooth. Add eggs, lemon oil, and lemon zest, and continue beating for 2 to 3 minutes until mixture is light and

fluffy. Add the ricotta and beat in well. Lower the speed and gently stir in the flour mixture until it forms a moist dough.

3. Use a small cookie scoop or your hands to form dough into 1½-inch balls. Place balls on parchment-paper-lined baking sheets about 1 inch apart. Refrigerate for 20 minutes.

4. Bake for 15 to 17 minutes, rotating sheets halfway through baking time, until the cookies are barely colored. Let cookies cool 1 minute on baking sheets, then transfer to cooling racks to cool completely.

5. For the glaze, whisk egg whites in a medium-size bowl until foamy. Add the powdered sugar, lemon juice, and lemon oil until well combined. Brush a thin layer of icing over the cookies. Let the icing set.

Makes about 4 dozen cookies

SANDIES
Recipe by Lisa Bisson

You will need:

  1 cup butter, room temperature

  ⅓ cup granulated sugar

  2 teaspoons water

  2 teaspoons vanilla

  2 cups flour

  1 cup walnuts or pecans, chopped

  ½ cup powdered sugar

Preheat oven to 325°

1. In a large mixing bowl, cream together butter and granulated sugar, using an electric mixer on high speed. Add water and vanilla; mix well. Add flour and nuts. Chill for 3 to 4 hours. Shape into 1-inch balls and place on parchment-paper-lined baking sheet.

2. Bake for about 20 minutes. Let cool for 2 to 3 minutes, then roll in powdered sugar to coat. Place on wire rack to cool completely.

Makes 3 dozen cookies

MOLASSES GINGER SNAPS
Recipe by Kris Gilbert

You will need:

  4 cups all-purpose flour

  2 teaspoons baking soda

  2 teaspoons ground cinnamon

  2 teaspoons ground cloves

  2 teaspoons ground ginger

  1½ cups shortening, no substitutions

  2 cups granulated sugar, plus ¼ cup extra for rolling

  2 eggs

  ½ cup molasses

Preheat oven to 375°

1. In a small bowl, sift together flour, soda, cinnamon, cloves, and ginger. Set aside.

2. In a large mixing bowl, beat shortening and 2 cups sugar together using an electric mixer on high speed. Beat in eggs and molasses, and as much flour mixture as possible. Stir in the rest.

3. Roll into even-size balls, and roll balls into extra ¼-cup of sugar. Place on a parchment-paper-lined baking sheet about 2 inches apart.

4. Bake for 12 to 13 minutes, or until golden brown.

Makes 5 dozen

CHOCOLATE CRACKLE-TOP COOKIES
Recipe by Veronique Deblois

You will need:

  1½ cups semi-sweet chocolate chips

  1½ cups all-purpose flour

  1½ teaspoons baking powder

  ¼ teaspoon salt

  1 cup granulated sugar

  6 tablespoons butter, room temperature

  1½ teaspoons vanilla

  2 large eggs

  1 cup powdered sugar

Preheat oven to 350°

1. Microwave 1 cup chocolate chips for 1 minute on medium power. Stir. Microwave at 10-second intervals until completely melted.

2. In a small bowl, sift together flour, baking powder, and salt.

3. In a large mixing bowl, beat sugar, butter, and vanilla using an electric mixer on high speed. Add melted chocolate until well blended. Incorporate eggs, one at a time. Gradually incorporate flour mixture in the chocolate mixture. Stir in remaining ½ cup chocolate chips. Chill until firm, about 30 minutes.

4. Shape cooled dough into 1½-inch balls. Place powdered sugar in a shallow dish and roll dough balls into it to cover completely. Place balls onto ungreased cookie sheets.

5. Bake for 13 to 15 minutes; the center of the cookies will not be firm but the edges will crack. Let cookies cool for 5 minutes on the cookie sheets, then transfer to a rack to completely cool.

Makes 2 dozen cookies

EVER GREENS

PISTACHIO-SPRINKLED CHOCOLATE CAKE

You will need:
CHOCOLATE CAKE

  1 cup of freshly brewed hot coffee

  6 ounces butter

  4 ounces bittersweet chocolate, finely chopped

  ¼ cup buttermilk

  1 teaspoon vanilla extract

  1 tablespoon instant espresso powder

  ½ cup whole-wheat pastry flour

  ½ cup unbleached all-purpose flour

  ½ cup unsweetened cocoa powder

  1 cup granulated sugar

  1 teaspoon baking powder

  ½ teaspoon cinnamon

  ½ teaspoon baking soda

  ½ teaspoon sea salt

2 eggs, slightly beaten

½ cup pistachio nuts, coarsely chopped

GANACHE

10 ounces bittersweet chocolate, finely chopped

12 ounces heavy cream

1 tablespoon butter

Preheat oven to 325°

1. Butter an 8-inch round cake pan and line with parchment paper.

2. In a small bowl, pour hot coffee over butter and chocolate. Stir together until melted. Add buttermilk, vanilla extract, and espresso powder. Set aside.

3. In a large mixing bowl, sift together flours, cocoa powder, sugar, baking powder, cinnamon, baking soda, and sea salt. Add eggs and coffee mixture, and mix until combined.

4. Pour batter into baking pan and bake for 20 to 25 minutes, or until a toothpick inserted in the center comes out clean. Let cool in pan on wire rack for 10 minutes. Remove from pan, and let cool completely on wire rack.

5. For the ganache, place chocolate in small bowl. Heat heavy cream until boiling and immediately pour over chopped chocolate. Let sit for a minute, then stir until combined. Add butter and stir until ganache becomes thick and creamy and fully mixed. Let sit for 10 to 15 minutes until thickened. Pour over top of cooled cake and let drip down the sides. Sprinkle with freshly chopped pistachio nuts.

GREEN TEA CHRISTMAS TREE COOKIES

You will need:

¾ cup powdered sugar

5 ounces unsalted butter, chilled and cut into cubes

1 ¾ cup all-purpose flour

3 large egg yolks

1 ½ tablespoons powdered green Matcha tea

Preheat oven to 350°

1. Whisk the powdered sugar and green tea together in a small bowl; set aside.

2. In the bowl of a stand mixer fitted with a paddle attachment, combine butter and tea mixture. Mix until smooth and light in color. Add the flour and mix until well combined. Add the egg yolks and mix just until the eggs are fully incorporated and a mass forms. (For dark green cookies, add two drops of evergreen-color icing gel when you add the egg yolks.)

3. Using your hands, form the dough into a disk, wrap in plastic wrap, and chill in the refrigerator for about 30 minutes or until firm.

4. On an lightly floured surface, roll the dough out to ½-inch thickness. Cut with a Christmas tree-shaped cookie cutter. Place the cookie on a parchment-paper-lined pan.

5. Bake for 12 to 15 minutes, or until slightly golden around the edges.

Makes 2 dozen cookies

CHRISTMAS PRESENT

LINDA'S MUM'S ENGLISH-IRISH TRIFLE

You will need:

1 package of white cake mix, baked (or 1 prepared pound cake from the grocery store)

1 package of strawberry gelatin, prepared but not completely set

3 cups fresh or canned fruit, cut up and juices reserved

2 cups Bird's Eye custard, prepared according to the directions and cooled

1 cup heavy whipping cream, beaten with an electric mixer until peaks form and the cream is set

1. Fill the bottom of a glass bowl or trifle dish with cubed pieces of cake.

2. Spoon the slightly runny gelatin over the cake, and layer the fruit and some of the fruit juices on top.

3. Pour the custard over the fruit and top with fresh, whipped cream. It's best to make this slowly, letting each layer soak in and set before adding the next. You don't want it too soggy or too dry. Store it in the refrigerator up to a week.

Makes 6 to 8 servings

IN THE PINK

PEPPERMINT MELTIES
Recipe by Koralee Teichroeb

You will need:

4 ½ cups confectioner's sugar

½ cup butter, softened

2 tablespoons cream

1 ½ teaspoons of peppermint extract

Liquid food coloring

1. Line baking sheet with parchment paper.

2. In the bowl of an electric mixer fitted with a paddle attachment, combine confectioner's sugar, butter, cream, and peppermint extract. Mix until they form a small ball.

3. Divide the dough into three portions and form each one into a ball. To color the mixture, add one drop of food coloring into one portion, kneading into dough evenly. Continue adding more coloring until desired shade. Repeat using a different color for each remaining portion.

4. Roll the dough into ½- to 1-inch-diameter ropes. Cut each rope into desired size pieces.

5. Arrange the pieces on the parchment paper and let sit uncovered overnight. Once dry, store in an airtight container.

ICE CREAM TOWERS

You will need:

    6 molds, such as water goblets

    ½ cup pistachios, coarsely chopped

    1 cup dried sweetened cranberries

    ½ cup slivered almonds, toasted

    1 teaspoon of ground cinnamon

    8 cups vanilla ice cream, softened

    For the topping, you will need:

    7 ounces white chocolate

    Dash of pink food coloring

    ¼ cup pistachios, chopped

    Pink sprinkles

1. Combine pistachios, cranberries, almonds and cinnamon together.

2. Stir into softened ice cream until well mixed.

3. Spoon mixture into the molds, making sure to level the top. Cover with plastic wrap. Freeze at least 5 hours or overnight, until set.

4. Line a baking tray with parchment paper.

5. Place a warm towel around the moulds to soften ice cream. Invert moulds onto the tray. Ice cream should just slide right out and onto tray. Pop tray into the freezer to firm the ice cream for at least 20 minutes.

6. While ice cream is firming, make the topping. In a glass bowl over simmering water, stir white chocolate until melted and smooth. Add a small dash of pink food coloring into the chocolate, stirring until well blended.

7. Remove the ice cream from freezer and place on individual serving plates. Top each one with the melted chocolate and sprinkle with pink sprinkles. Serve immediately.

SUNRISE BREAKFAST

MORNING TROPICAL SALAD

You will need:

    1 large ripe mango, diced

    3 whole oranges, peeled and cut into sections

    2 cups fresh pineapple, cubed

    2 cups cantaloupe, cubed

    4 kiwi, peeled and cut into quarters

    2 tablespoons lemon juice

    2 teaspoons honey

1. In a medium-size stainless-steel bowl, combine all fruit, lemon juice, and honey. Mix well and cover.

2. Refrigerate for 1 hour before serving to let the flavors blend.

RASPBERRY MIMOSA

You will need:

    ½ cup brandy

    3 tablespoons clear raspberry brandy

    4 ½ tablespoons granulated sugar

    1 cup fresh raspberries, mashed

    1 bottle chilled Champagne or sparkling white wine

    Whole fresh raspberries for garnish

1. In a glass pitcher, stir brandies and sugar in a medium bowl. Add mashed raspberries and let stand 1 hour at room temperature; then strain.

2. Divide brandy mixture among 6 flutes, adding several whole raspberries to each glass.

3. Pour Champagne over fruit-brandy mixture and serve.

A SWEET LIFE

SNOWFLAKE COOKIES

You will need:

    1 cup butter, softened

    1 cup sugar

    2 large eggs

    2 teaspoons vanilla extract

    3 ¼ cups all-purpose flour

    2 teaspoons baking powder

    ½ teaspoon salt

Preheat oven to 350°

1. In a large bowl, beat butter and sugar using an electric mixer on high speed until fluffy. Beat in eggs and vanilla.

2. In a medium bowl, combine flour, baking powder, and salt. Gradually add to sugar mixture, beating until smooth. Wrap dough in heavy-duty plastic wrap, and refrigerate 1 hour.

3. On a lightly floured surface, roll out dough to ¼-inch thickness. Cut with assorted snowflake cookie cutters and place 2 inches apart on parchment-paper-lined baking sheets. Chill pans of dough for 15 minutes.

4. Bake for 10 minutes, or until edges are very lightly browned. Let cool for 2 minutes on baking sheet. Remove from pans and cool completely on wire racks. Frost and decorate with royal icing in desired colors. (See page 234 for Royal Icing recipe.)

COOL, CALM & COLLECTED

EDAMAME-PESTO BRUSCHETTA

You will need:

- 1 baguette, sliced
- 8 ounces olive oil
- Salt and pepper to taste
- 16 ounces shelled whole fresh edamame
- 6 ounces fresh basil leaves
- 3 ounces Parmesan, grated
- 2 garlic cloves
- 2 ounces Parmesan, shaved into curls
- Black and white sesame seeds, toasted in a dry sauté pan

Preheat oven to 350°

1. Place sliced baguette on a parchment-paper-lined sheet pan. Brush olive oil over slices and season with salt and pepper. Bake 5 to 10 minutes, or until golden and crispy.

2. Set aside about 20 whole edamame to use for garnish. In food processor, combine the rest of the edamame, basil, grated Parmesan, and garlic; process until it becomes a paste. Slowly add olive oil and process until smooth.

3. Top each slice of baguette with 1 tablespoon of pesto. Garnish with whole edamame, Parmesan curls, and toasted black and white sesame seeds.

Makes about 8 servings

CHEESY FLATBREAD WITH CRANBERRY-SPINACH SALAD

You will need:

- 1 package refrigerated pizza dough, divided in half
- ⅔ cup fresh prepared Alfredo Sauce, divided in half
- ¾ cup shredded mozzarella cheese, divided in half

Preheat oven to 375°

1. On a lightly floured surface, flatten each ball of dough, starting in the center and working outwards. Use your fingertips to press the dough until it is ½-inch thick. Let the dough relax 5 minutes, and then continue to stretch it until it reaches the desired diameter of 10 to 12 inches. Place dough on a lightly oiled cookie sheet.

2. Brush the top of the dough with olive oil and top with sauce and cheese. Bake one pizza at a time for 10 to 15 minutes or until lightly browned and bubbly.

3. Remove from oven and top with spinach cranberry salad.

CRANBERRY SPINACH SALAD

You will need:

- 1 tablespoon butter
- ¾ cup cooked prosciutto, shredded
- 1 pound baby spinach leaves
- ½ cup fresh cranberries
- ½ cup granulated sugar
- 2 teaspoons minced onion
- ¼ teaspoon paprika
- ¼ cup white wine vinegar
- ¼ cup cider vinegar
- ½ cup vegetable oil
- salt and pepper to taste

1. In a large bowl, combine the spinach and cranberries. Set aside.

2. In a medium bowl, whisk together the sugar, onion, paprika, vinegars, and vegetable oil.

3. Drizzle dressing over the spinach-cranberry mixture and toss. Top hot pizzas with heaping mounds of salad and sprinkle with prosciutto. Serve immediately.

LOBSTER CHOWDER

You will need:

- 2 ½ cups cooked lobster meat, chopped
- 2 bacon slices, chopped
- 1 cup green onions, chopped
- 1 teaspoon Hungarian sweet paprika
- ½ teaspoon ground cumin
- 2 cups baking potato, peeled and diced
- 1 cup half-and-half
- 2 teaspoons granulated sugar
- ½ teaspoon salt
- ¼ teaspoon ground white pepper
- 2 cups fresh corn kernels (about 4 ears)
- Chopped fresh chives (optional)
- 4 cups chicken stock (or 2 cups chicken stock and 2 cups clam juice)

1. Cook bacon in a large Dutch oven over medium-high heat until crisp. Add onions; sauté for 2 minutes. Stir in paprika and cumin, and cook for one minute. Add potato and stock; bring to a boil. Cook for 15 minutes or until potato is tender. Remove from heat.

2. Stir in lobster meat, half-and-half, sugar, salt, and pepper. Cover and refrigerate 1 hour.

3. Return pan to stove and bring to simmer on low heat. Add corn; cook for 5 minutes.

Makes about 8 servings

DOUBLE CHOCOLATE COOKIES

You will need:

- 8 ounces semisweet chocolate, roughly chopped
- 4 tablespoons butter
- ⅔ cup all-purpose flour
- ½ teaspoon baking powder
- ½ teaspoon salt
- 2 large eggs
- ¾ cup light-brown sugar, packed
- 1 teaspoon vanilla extract

1 package (12 ounces) double-chocolate chips

Preheat oven to 350°

1. Combine chopped chocolate and butter in a microwave-safe bowl and heat in the microwave on high until almost melted. Stir the chocolate every 20 seconds.

2. In small mixing bowl, whisk together flour, baking powder, and salt. Set aside.

3. In a large mixing bowl, beat eggs, brown sugar, and vanilla using an electric mixer on high speed until light and fluffy. Reduce speed to low and beat in melted chocolate. Mix in flour mixture until just combined. Stir in chocolate chips.

4. Drop heaping tablespoons of dough onto parchment-paper-lined baking sheets about 2 inches apart. Bake 12 to 15 minutes or until cookies are shiny and crackly yet soft in the centers. Cool on the cookie sheet. Serve immediately; do not store.

PERFECT CHOCOLATE GANACHE—TWO WAYS

Chocolate Tarts with Gingersnap Crust and Chocolate Mousse

CHOCOLATE GANACHE

You will need:

    12 ounces dark chocolate, chopped

    4 tablespoons butter, room temperature

    1 cup heavy cream

    ¼ cup corn syrup

    ¼ teaspoon vanilla

1. In a medium-size, heat-proof bowl, place chocolate pieces. In a medium saucepan over medium heat, warm the cream until it comes to a boil. Remove from heat and pour over chocolate. Shake the bowl gently to combine the chocolate and cream, and then let it sit, undisturbed, for 2 minutes.

2. Stir the mixture with a whisk until it is smooth and allow it to cool. When thick and creamy, pour it into tart pans filled with baked gingersnap pie crusts.

GINGERSNAP PIE CRUST

You will need:

    2 cups gingersnap cookies, finely ground

    3 tablspoons granulated sugar

    ½ teaspoon ground ginger

    6 tablespoons butter, melted

Preheat oven to 350°

1. Combine all ingredients in medium bowl. Using clean hands, press into four greased 3-inch fluted tart pans with removeable bottoms.

2. Bake for 10 minutes, or until crust is set. Remove from oven and cool completely before filling.

CHOCOLATE MOUSSE

To turn the ganache into a light and creamy mousse, pour the slightly cooled ganache into a large mixing bowl and whip on high speed using a stand mixer or electric mixer on high speed. Whip it on high speed until stiff peaks form. Using a spoon or pastry bag, transfer the mousse to serving dishes and serve immediately.

APRÈS TREE

CHEESE FONDUE

You will need:

    2 cups milk

    1 Tablespoon Worcestershire sauce

    2 teaspoons dry mustard

    1 clove garlic, peeled and crushed

    3 tablespoons all-purpose flour

    6 cups shredded cheddar cheese

1. In a medium saucepan, whisk together milk, Worcestershire sauce, mustard, garlic, and flour. Cook over low heat until the mixture reaches a simmer. Do not boil.

2. Stir in cheese. Heat until the cheese has melted.

3. Transfer to a fondue pot to keep warm.

CHOCOLATE FONDUE

You will need:

    1 ½ cups heavy cream

    1 pound good-quality semi-sweet or bittersweet chocolate, chopped

    Pinch of sea salt

1. Pour the cream into a medium-size heavy saucepan, and heat over low heat until the cream reaches a simmer. Do not boil.

2. Add the chocolate and sea salt. Stir until melted.

3. Transfer to a fondue pot to keep warm.

SPICED CIDER

You will need:

    6 cups apple cider

    ½ teaspoon whole cloves

    ¼ teaspoon ground nutmeg

    3 cinnamon sticks

1. In a large saucepan, heat ingredients to boiling over medium-high heat. Reduce heat; simmer uncovered for 10 minutes.

2. Strain mixture to remove cloves and cinnamon; serve.

templates

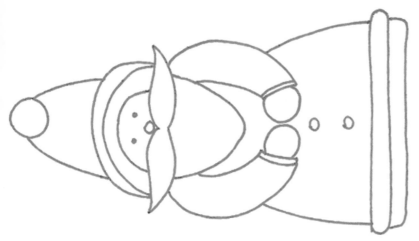

STORYBOOK HOLIDAY

FROSTING SANTA Copy and place pattern under parchment paper and pipe icing directly on parchment paper. Royal icing will provide a thin version and boiled icing will create a puffy version.

STORYBOOK HOLIDAY

Print on double-sided matte brochure paper. Cut out and wrap around tissue-wrapped tube filled with trinkets.

ANGELS

Cake stencil: Copy and cut out shape and small details.

This long strip is what is used as a support to keep the angel standing.

side view
of support.

ANGELS
Print on double-sided matte brochure paper and cut out with scissors.

ANGELS

Print on double-sided matte brochure paper and cut out with scissors. Glitter as desired using ModPodge®.

ANGELS

Copy onto double-sided matte brochure paper and cut out shape and small details.

RED AND WHITE DELIGHT

Paper petal wreath. Copy and cut out petal shape. Trace onto double-sided matte brochure paper. Make 100 petals for a 10" wreath. Attach to wreath form with straight pins.

RED AND WHITE DELIGHT
Copy onto double-sided matte brochure paper and cut out with scissors.

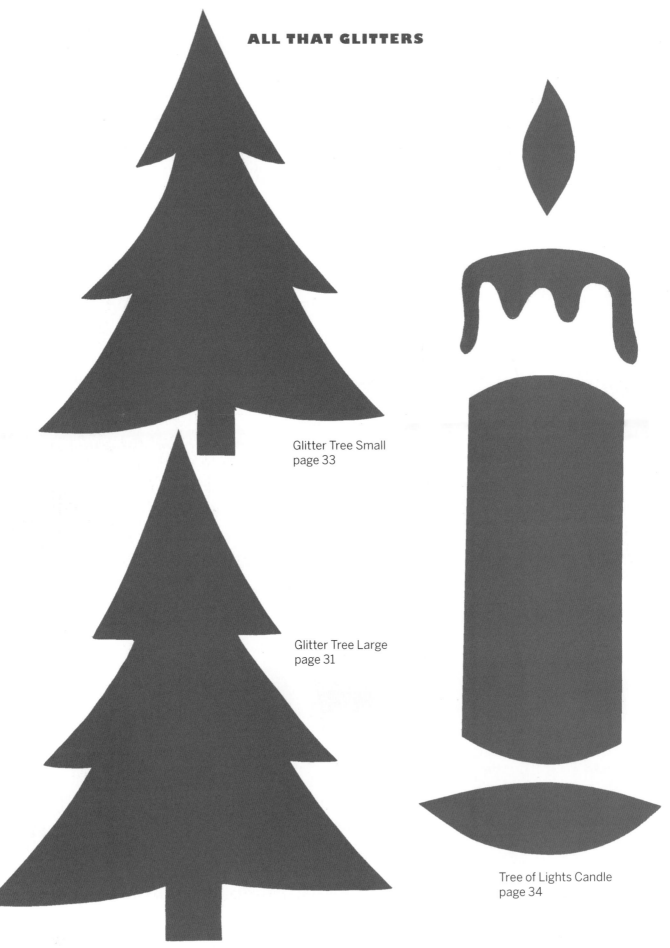

ALL THAT GLITTERS

Glitter Tree Small
page 33

Glitter Tree Large
page 31

Tree of Lights Candle
page 34

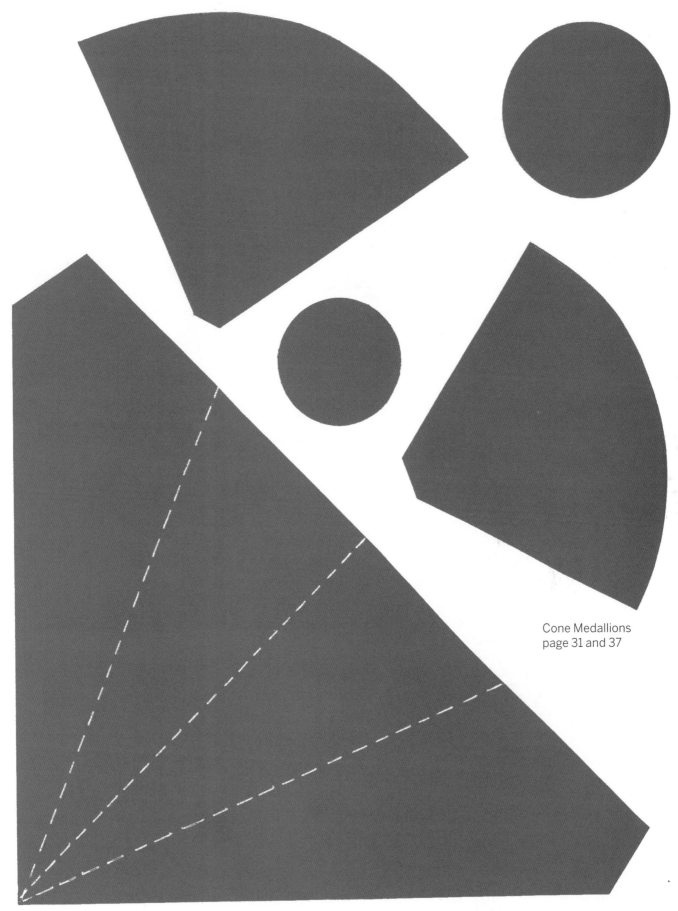

Cone Medallions
page 31 and 37

Wall Pocket
page 35

GIFTS FROM NATURE
Wreath: Copy onto double-sided matte
brochure paper and cut out with scissors.

SWEET LIFE
Copy onto double-sided
matte brochure paper.

Home Plate
page 231

Milk Puppets
page 229

Cute Sippers
page 232

Merry
Christmas

**SUNRISE
BREAKFAST**
Copy and cut out.

SUNRISE BREAKFAST
Copy and use for ornaments and tags.

resources

The materials and ingredients for the recipes and projects in this issue of **HOLIDAY** with Matthew Mead can be found at the following retail outlets:

CAKE AND COOKIE DECORATING
The Baker's Kitchen
TheBakersKitchen.net

Chandlers Cake and Candy Supplies
ChandlersCakeandCandy.com

Chef Tools Network, Inc
ChefTools.com

Fancy Flours
FancyFlours.com

Garnish
ThinkGarnish.com/store

Wilton
Wilton.com

CRAFTS
A.C. Moore Arts & Crafts
ACMoore.com

Anything In Stained Glass
AnythingInStainedGlass.com

Create For Less
CreateForLess.com

DIY Bangles
DIYBangles.com

Fiskars
Fiskars.com

JoAnn Fabric and Craft Stores
JoAnn.com

June Tailor, Inc.
JuneTailor.com

Michaels Stores
Michaels.com

Rustic Woodworking
RusticWoodworking.com

Scrapbook Online
Scrapbook.com

ENTERTAINING
Fish's Eddy
FishsEddy.com

HOME DÉCOR
Crate & Barrel
CrateAndBarrel.com

Curious Sofa
CuriousSofa.com

IKEA
Ikea.com

Luna Bazaar
LunaBazaar.com

Macy's
Macys.com

Matthew Mead Collection
Etsy.com/Shop/
MatthewMeadVintage

Pier 1 Imports
Pier1.com

Raised In Cotton
Raymore, MO

The Spotted Cod
Sandwich, MA

Target
Target.com

TJX Companies
HomeGoods.com

TJMaxx.com
MarshallsOnline.com

West Elm
WestElm.com

NATURE CRAFTS SUPPLIES
Attar Herbs and Spices
AttarHerbs.com

Lynch Creek Farm
LynchCreekWreaths.com

Maine Wreath Company
MaineWreathCo.com

Nature's Pressed Flowers
NaturesPressed.com

Seashell World
SeashellWorld.com

OFFICE SUPPLY
The Container Store
ContainerStore.com

Staples
Staples.com

TEMPLATES & RECIPES
HolidayWithMatthewMead.com

WRAPPING PAPERS AND PARTY SUPPLIES
Paper Mart
PaperMart.com

Paper Source
Paper-Source.com

Pearl River, Inc.
PearlRiver.com

PIKKU
PIKKUwares.com

Red River Paper
RedRiverCatalog.com

Vintage Paper Parade
Etsy.com/Shop/
VintagePaperParade

For more information about these projects or recipes, please visit our blogging friends at:

FOOD
Savour-Fare.com
BluebirdNotes.blogspot.com
TheBedlamOfBeefy.blogspot.com

CRAFTS
AmyBarickman.com
MatthewMeadStyle.com
NieNieDialogues.com
SwirlyDesigns.com

DECORATING
BrooklynLimestone.com
CheapDecorating.blogspot.com
CuriousSofa.blogspot.com
RaisedInCotton.typepad.com
ReStyledHome.ca
TheDecoratedTree.blogspot.com
VintagePaperParade.blogspot.com